THE OXHERD BOY

REGINA LINKE

THE OXHERD BOY

Parables of Love, Compassion, and Community

CLARKSON POTTER/PUBLISHERS

NEW YORK

*To my mom, who taught me
right from wrong, and my dad,
who showed me how to live
in a world that has both*

INTRODUCTION

"You'll never be a great *gongbi* artist."

Having grown up through a supportive American school system in the 90s, I found this verdict, delivered so definitively by my painting teacher in Taiwan, surprising and harsh. Though he continued to advise me that I'd have greater opportunities if I developed my own style separate from tradition, I didn't feel any better. It wasn't clear to me how I would change the direction of my career as an artist.

I was thirty-five years old, living in my parents' home again in a new city on the other side of the world. It was a place where I could navigate the matters of daily living but struggled to plumb the depths of cultural nuance. And it was here that my husband and I chose to raise our young son who was at an age where he demanded answers to some big questions on life and death, love and fear, fairness and forgiveness—basically, what it meant to be a human being. It was strange to be confronted with my own ignorance about such fundamental, universal topics; and it was in this crucible that I began *The Oxherd Boy*.

The three friends you'll meet—the ox, the oxherd boy, and the rabbit—take shape around the Three Harmonious Teachings, which are the pillars of Chinese philosophical thought. We first encounter the boy, a character inspired by Taoism. He looks at the world without judging right from wrong, accepting both as a source of balance in the world. The ox, a strong and simple character who views the world through a Buddhist lens, joins the boy's innocence with kindness. We all experience pain and suffering on this earth, and therefore, we are all capable of compassion. Lastly, the rabbit, representing Confucianism, comes into the fold. She is an active and industrious participant concerned with how we look after each other here on earth. Together, they help one another develop peaceful relationships with nature, their community of family and neighbors, and themselves.

As delightful as it's been to create this collection with my son in mind, what I didn't expect was how much the project would shape my own self-awareness and understanding. Working on *The Oxherd Boy* continues to inform and guide my own patterns as a parent, an emerging artist and author, and in general, a person engaged in the slow work of illuminating previously unexamined corners of her heart and mind.

As it would turn out, *The Oxherd Boy* became the book that I most needed to create for myself. But this world is for you, too. I hope you enjoy it as much as I have.

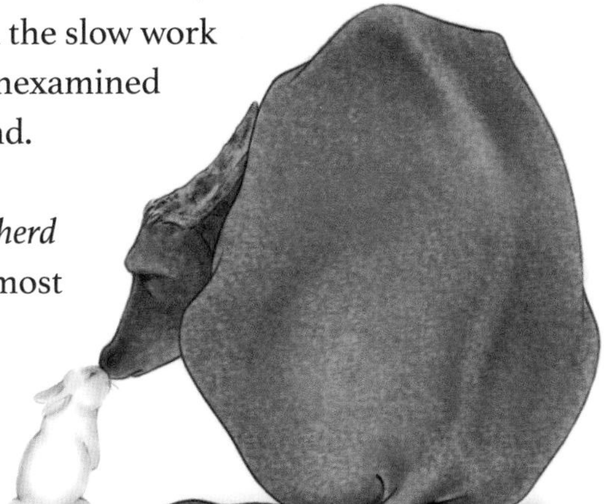

"I feel like a tiny, tiny drop
in such a big, big world."

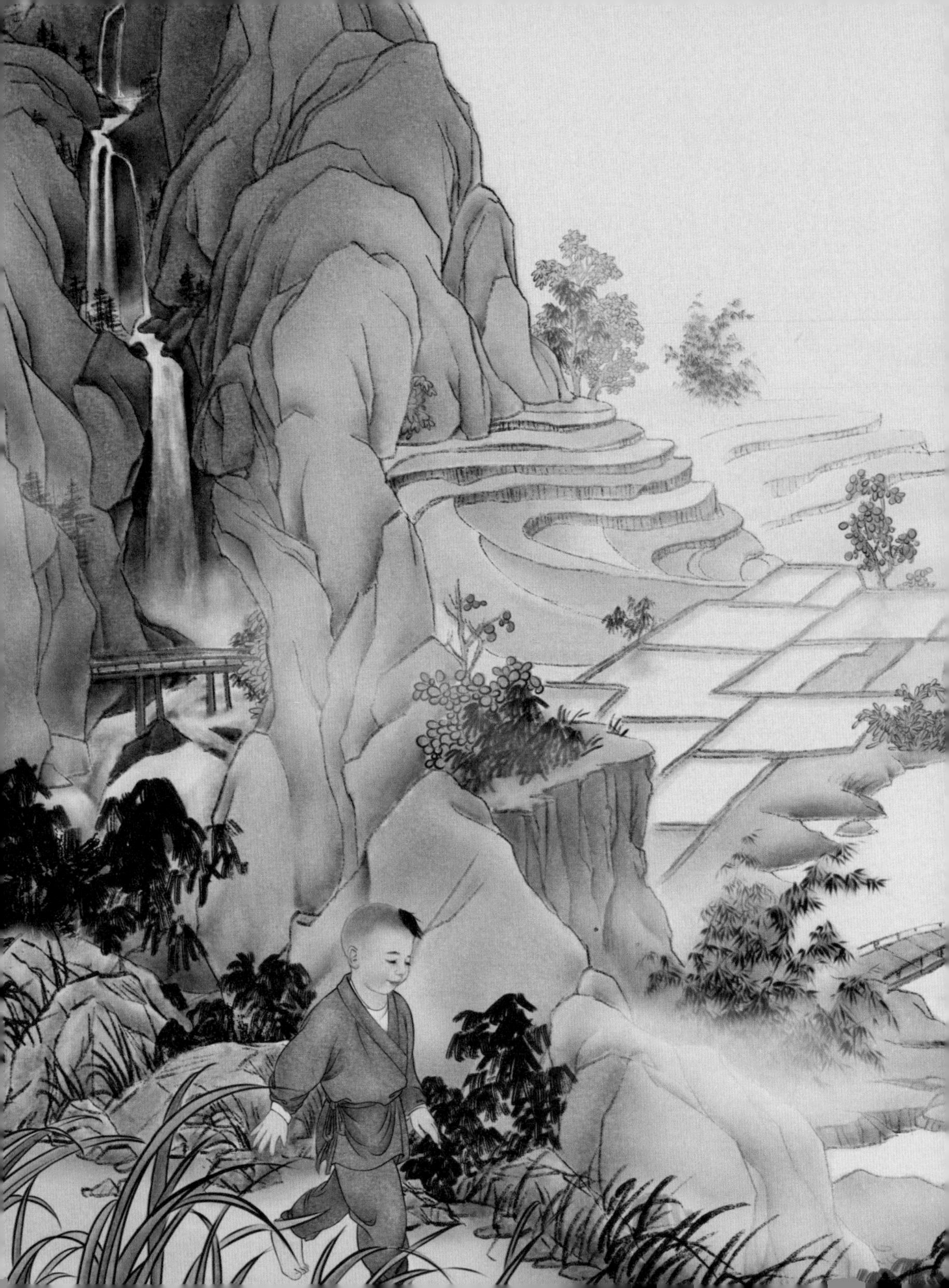

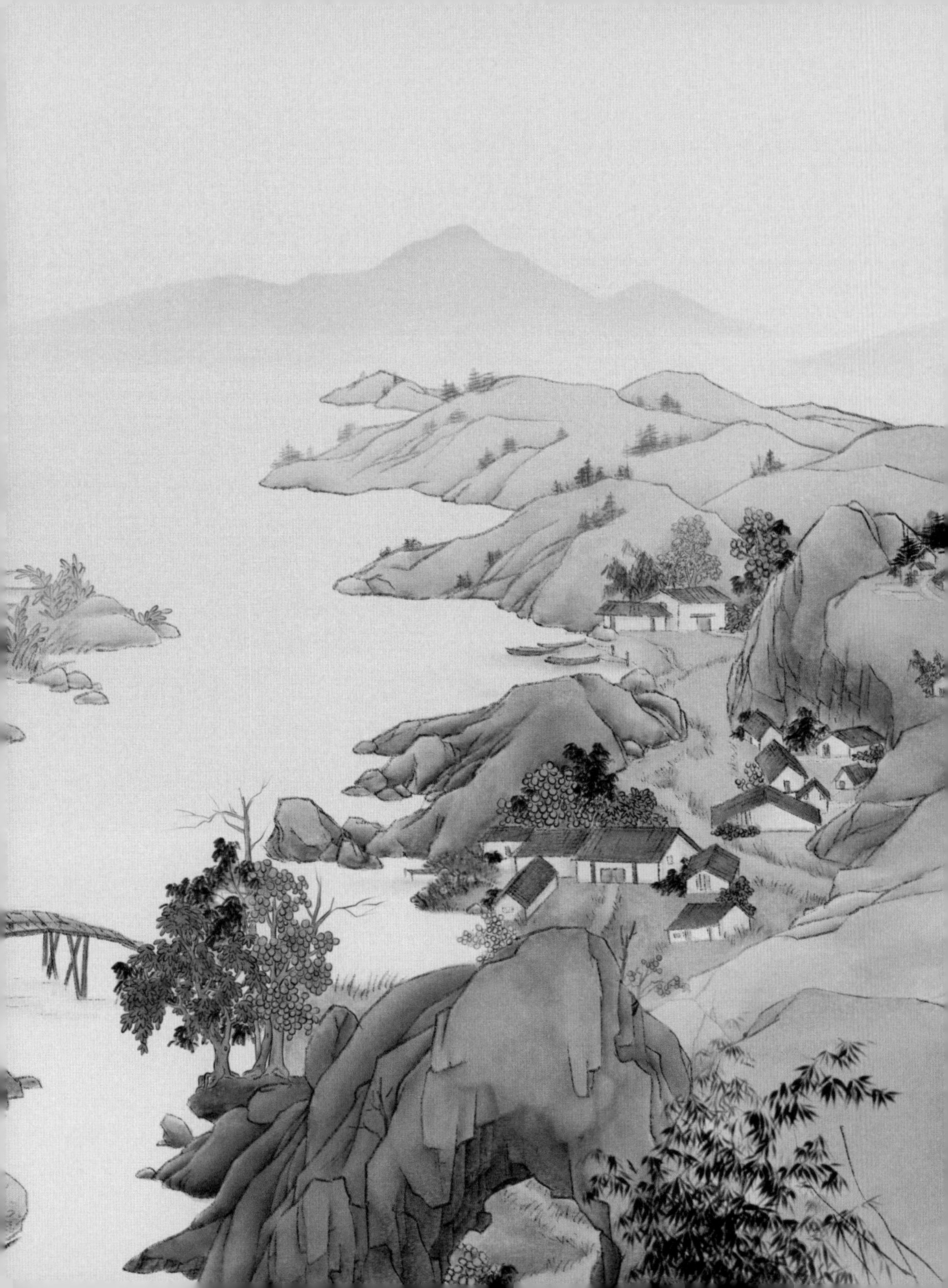

The boy looked up to find the family ox staring back at him. "Did your grandfather send you to bring me home today?" the ox asked him.

"Yes, but I'm scared," he replied.

"That's all right. Fear is natural, but kindness shall overcome."

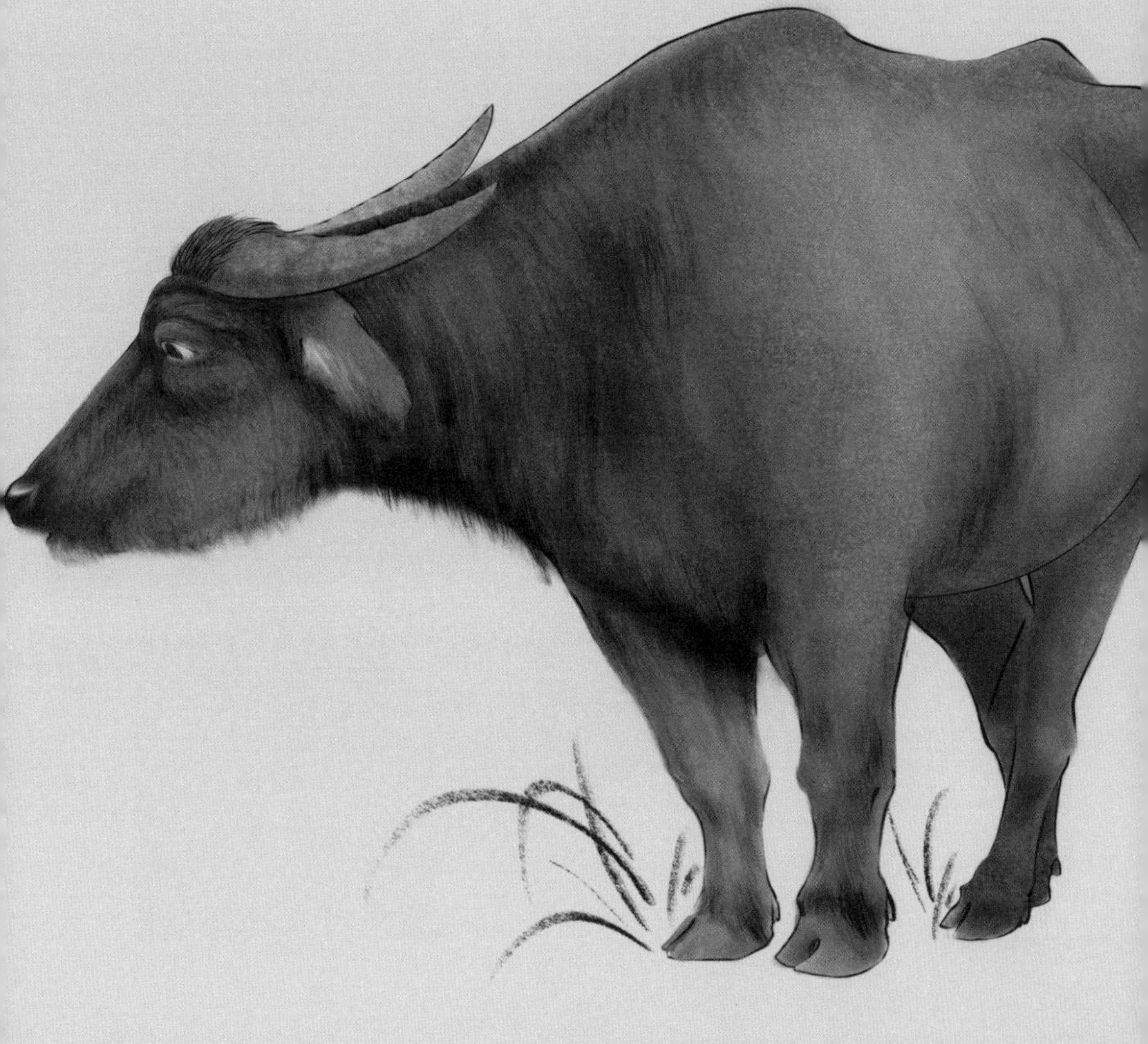

The boy struggled as he climbed up. "I can't," he cried.

The ox encouraged him, "You can. You need not rush. You need to breathe."

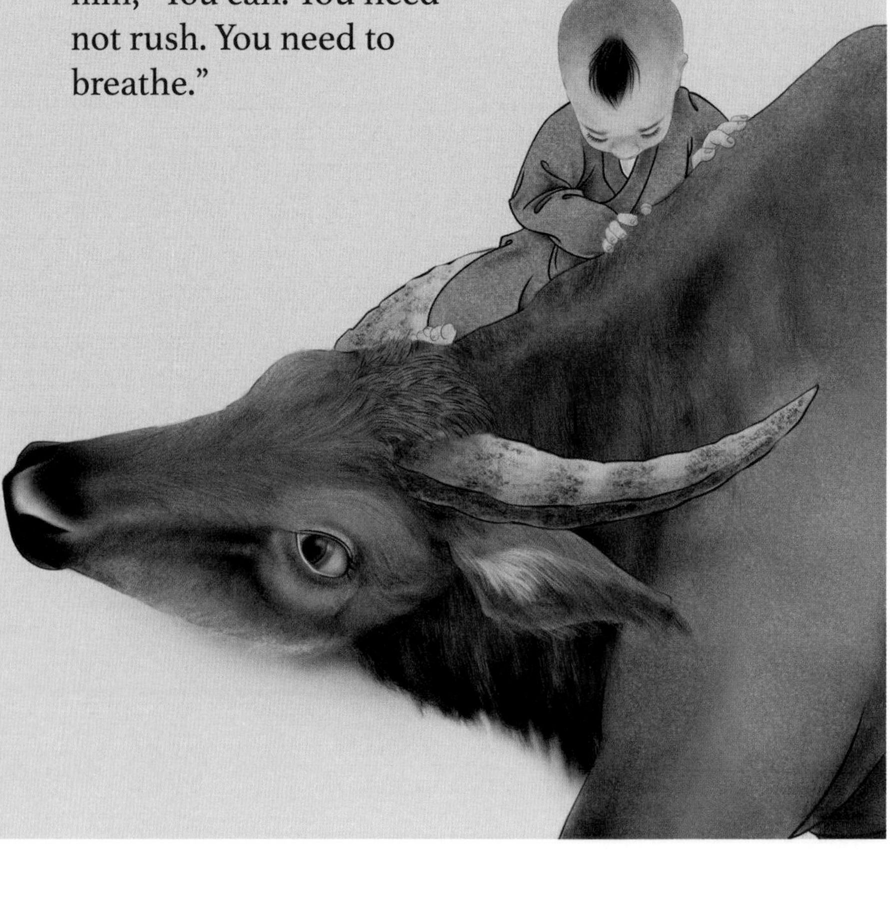

"The view is very different from up here."

"It often is," the ox agreed with a smile, and they started for home.

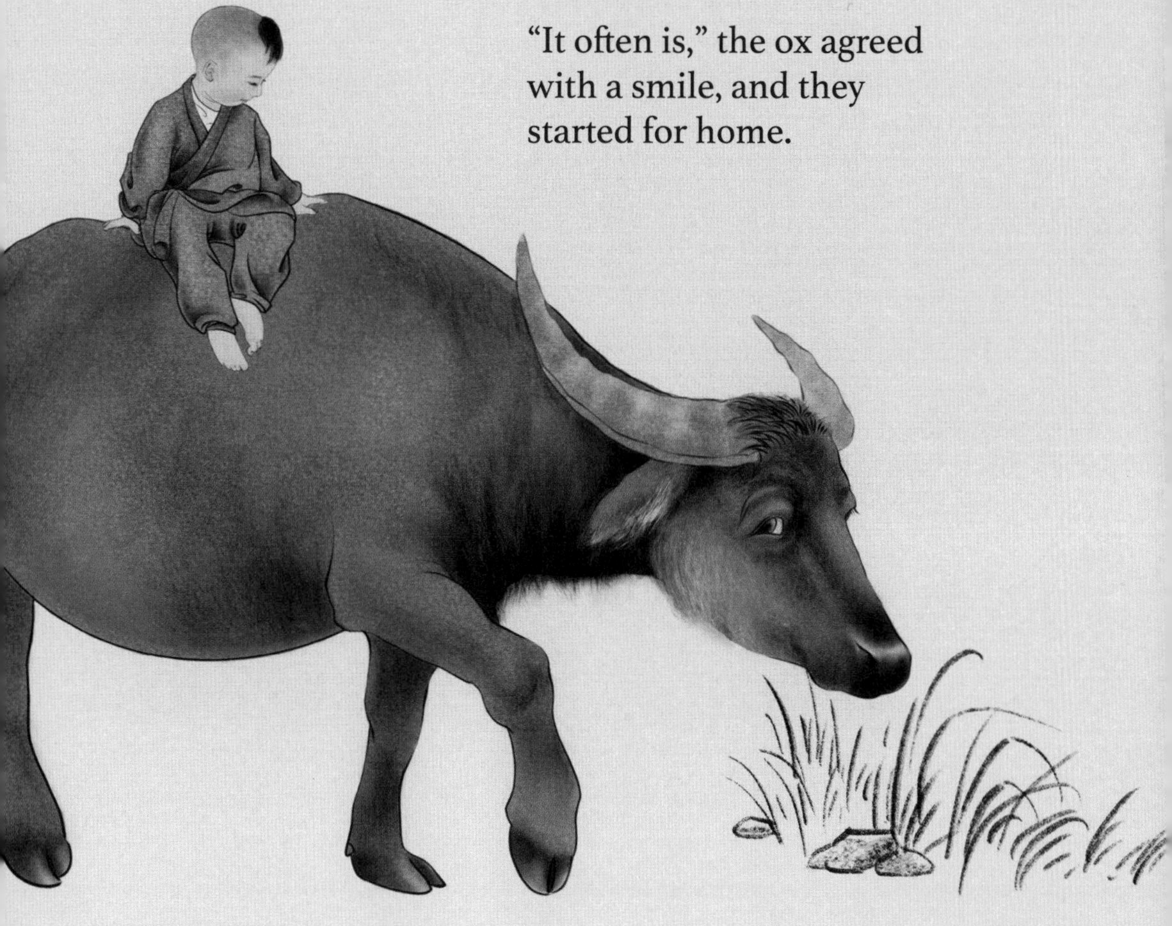

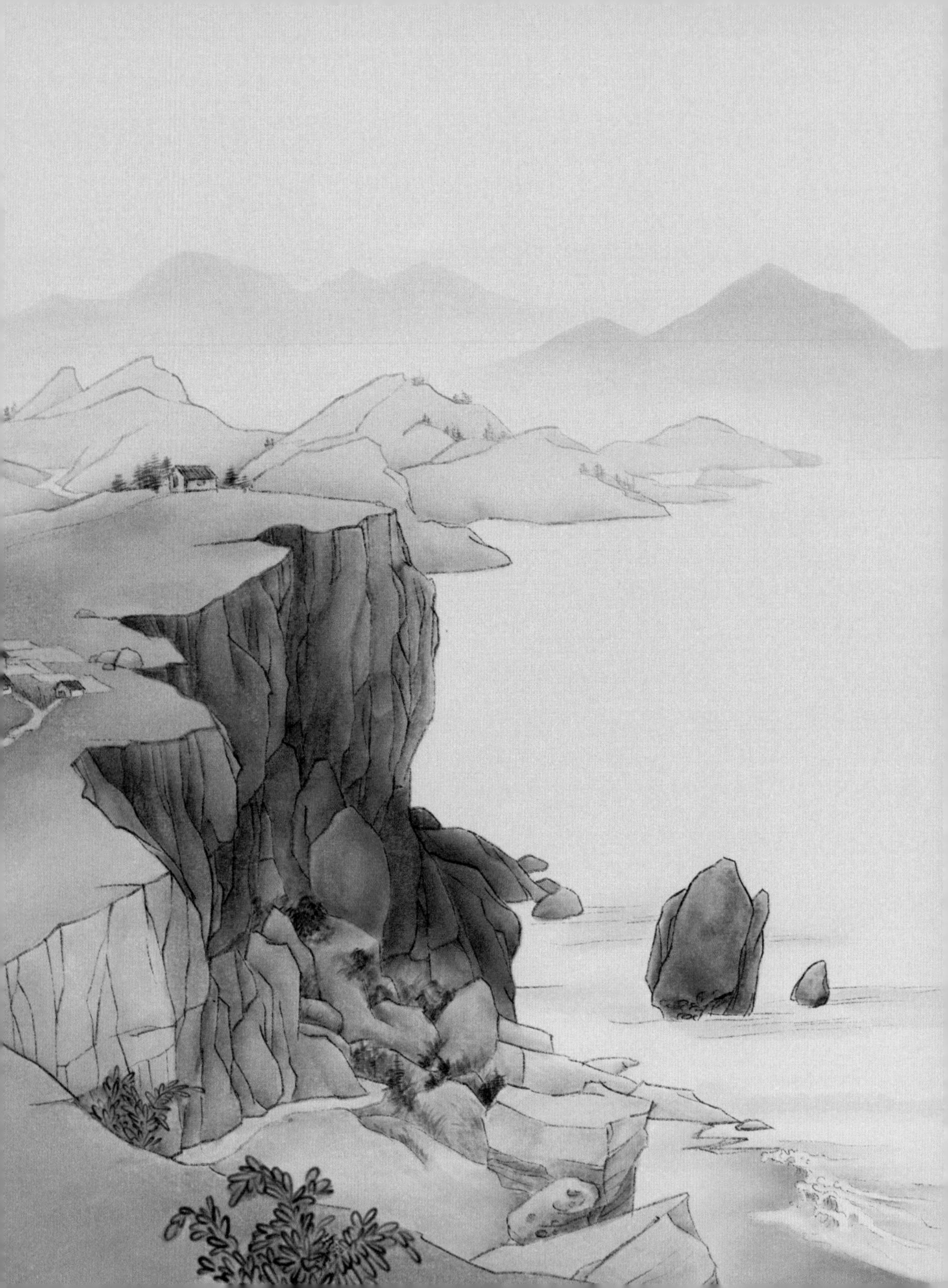

Life's greatest discoveries are
made by continually seeing
Home with fresh eyes.

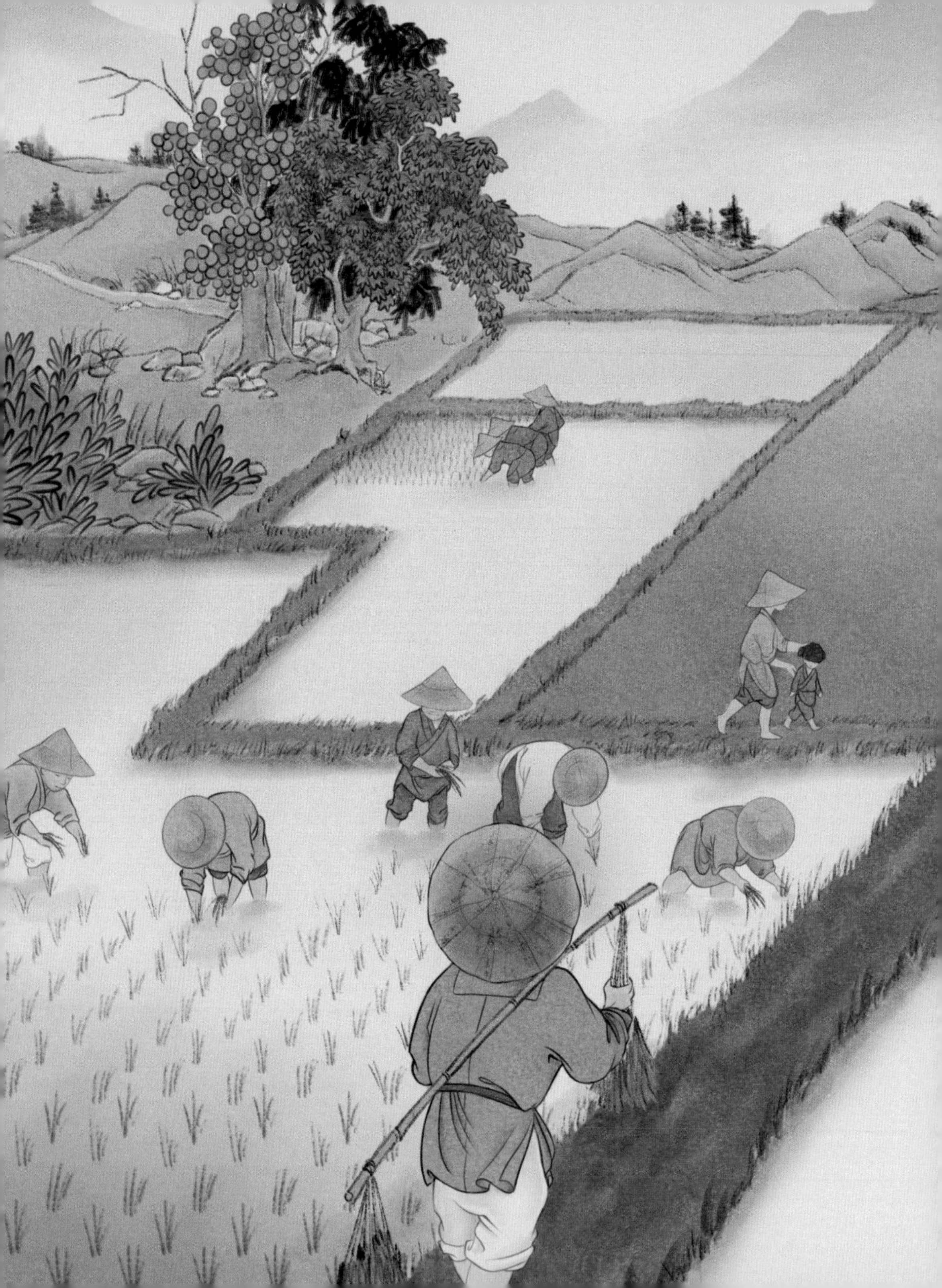

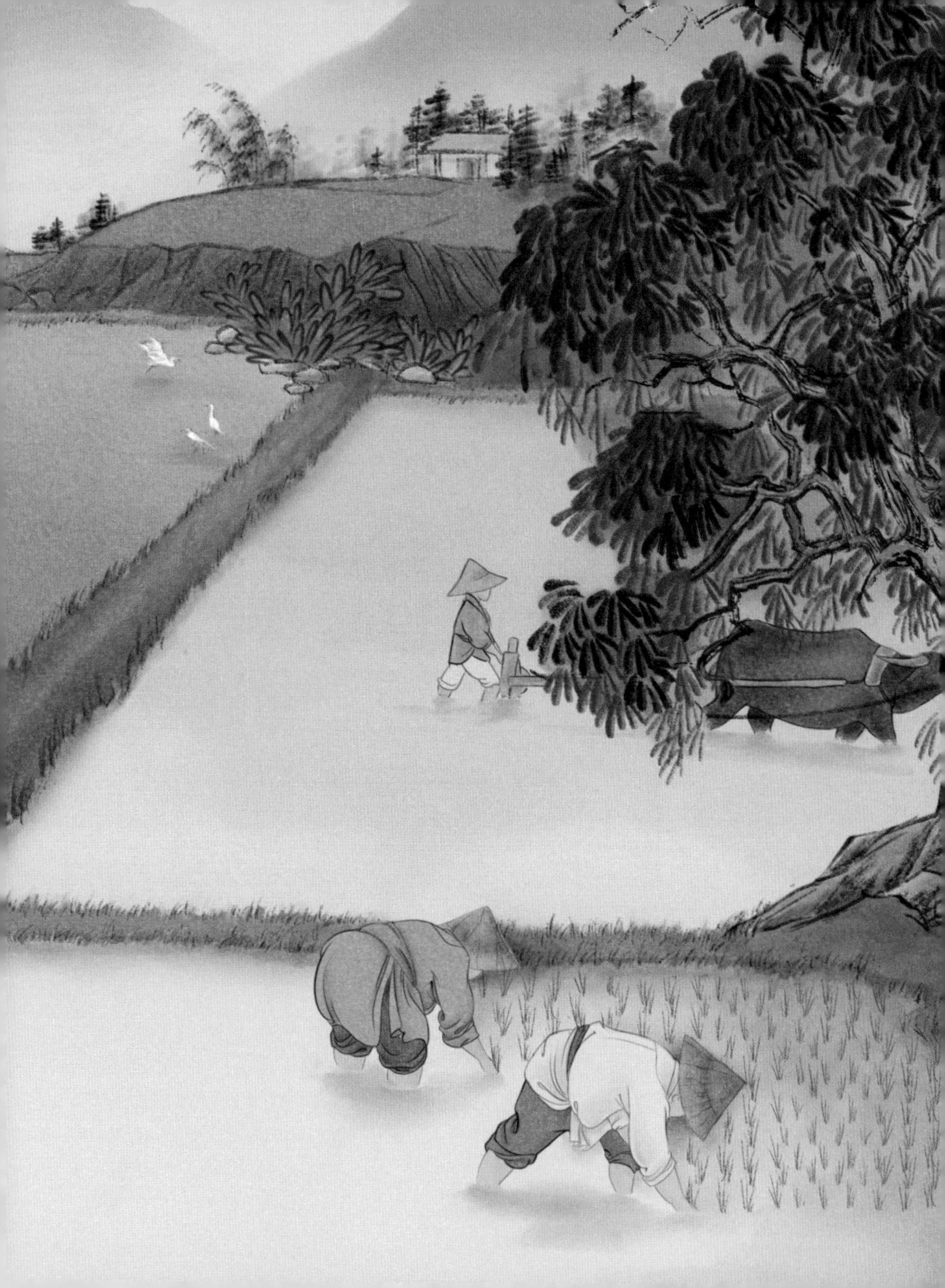

The work of planting
was new for the oxherd
boy. "This is hard," he
complained.

His grandfather nodded.
"Yes, but so is everything,
at least at first."

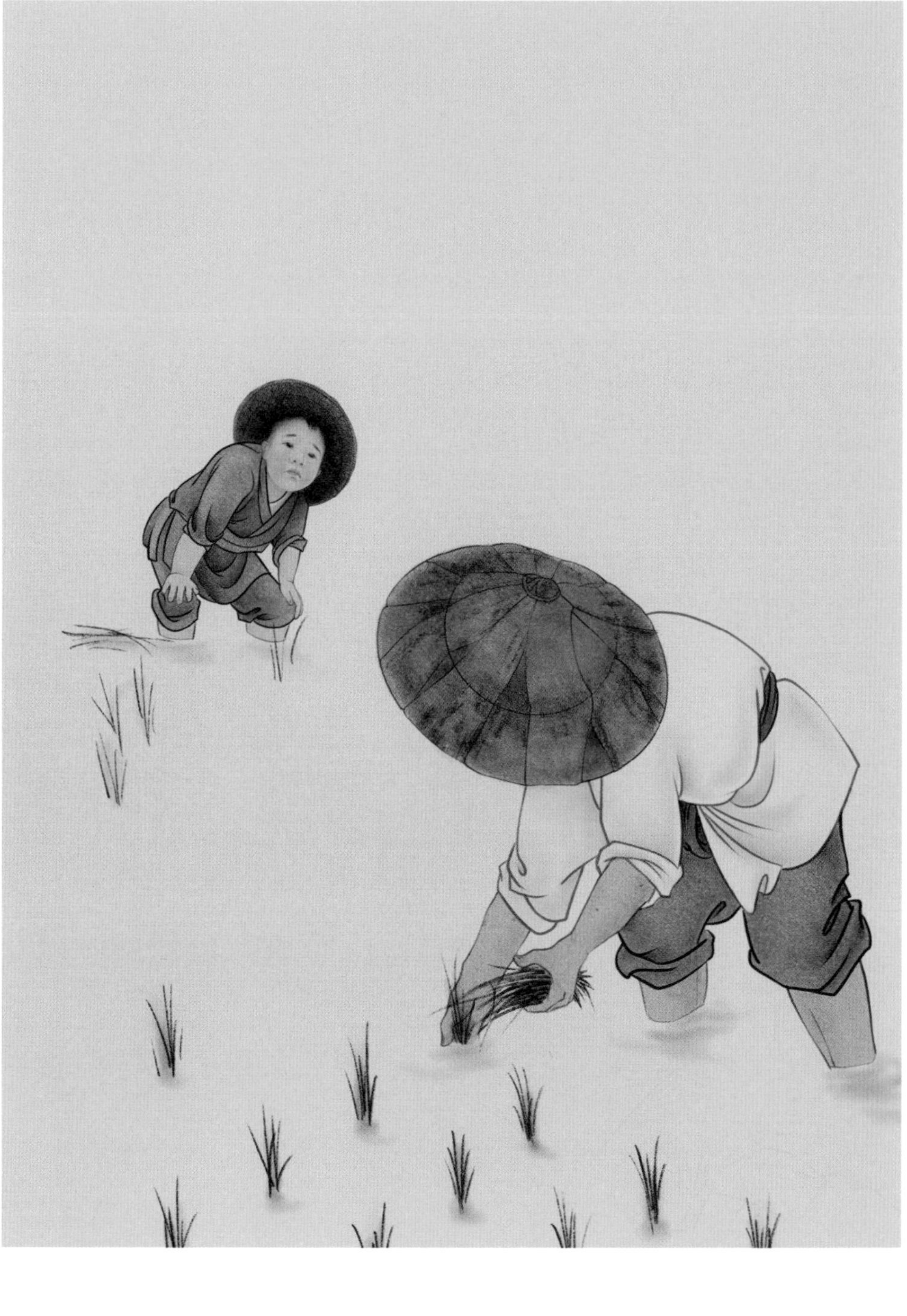

No one understood better than the ox. "Because I have suffered," he said,

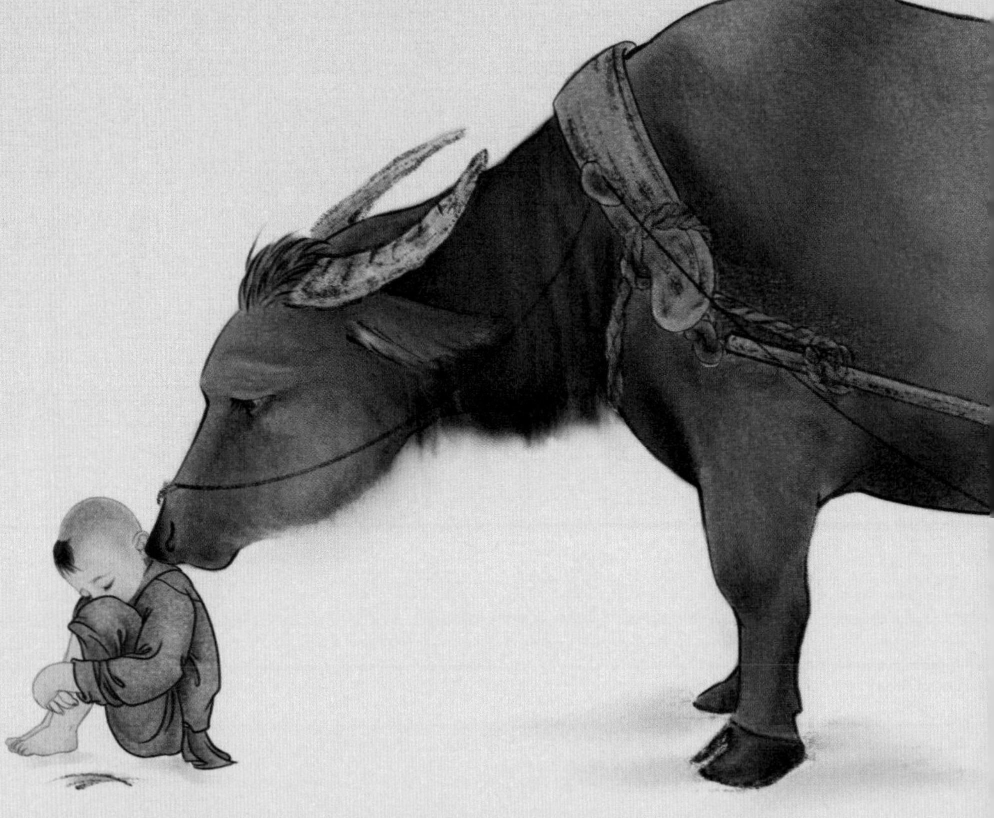

"I see your suffering,
and your pain is my pain."

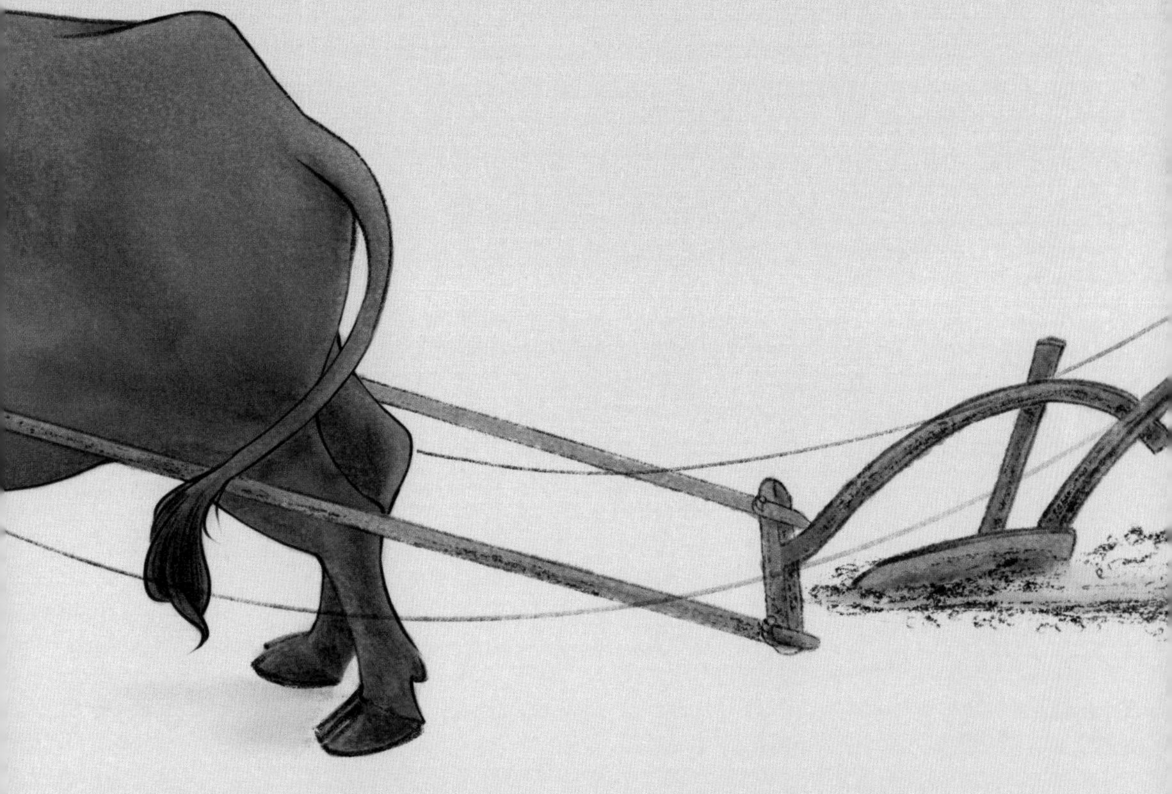

“Don’t you ever get tired of doing chores all day?” asked the boy.

“Of course,” the ox replied, “but then I remember that some people dream of having my life.”

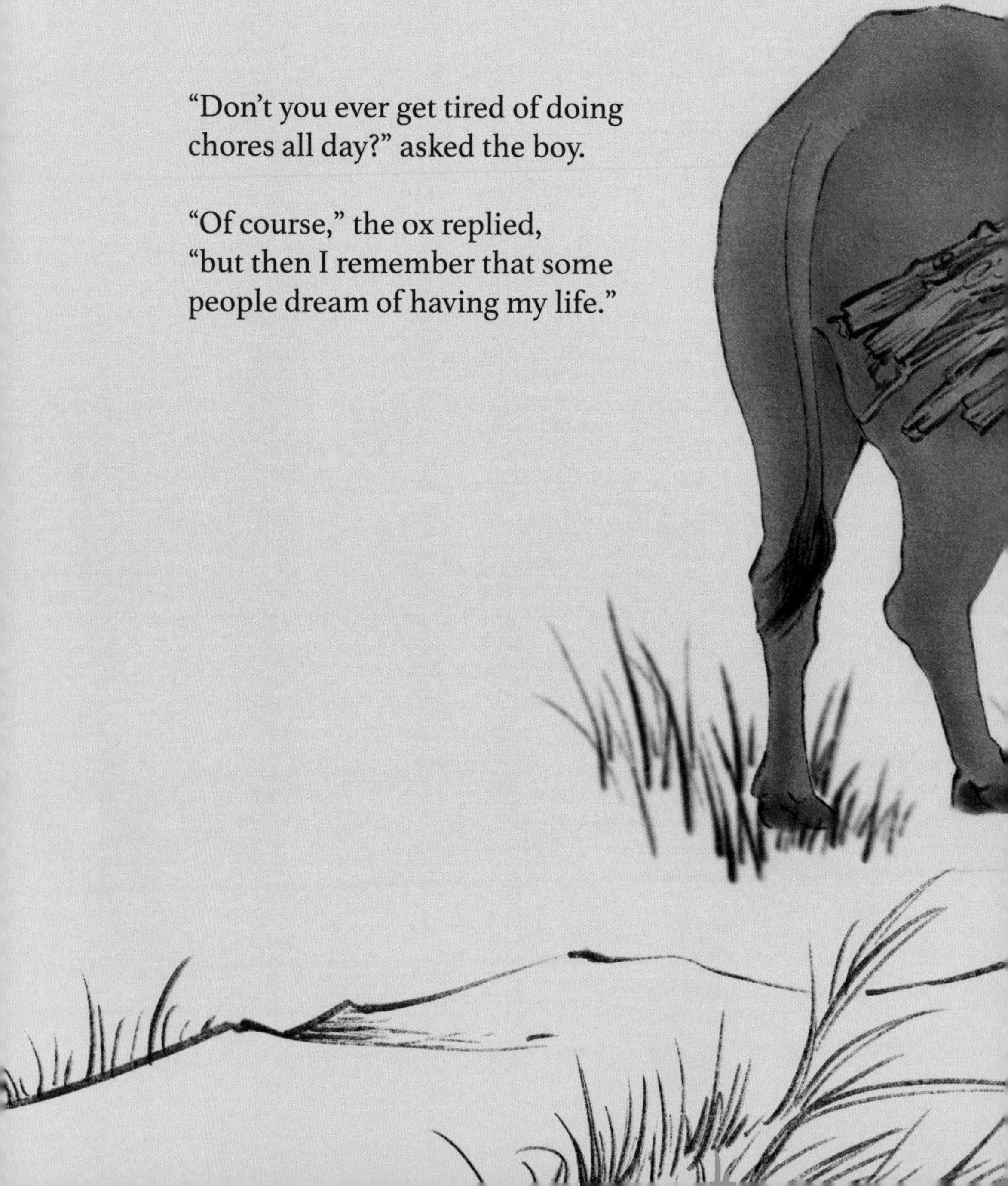

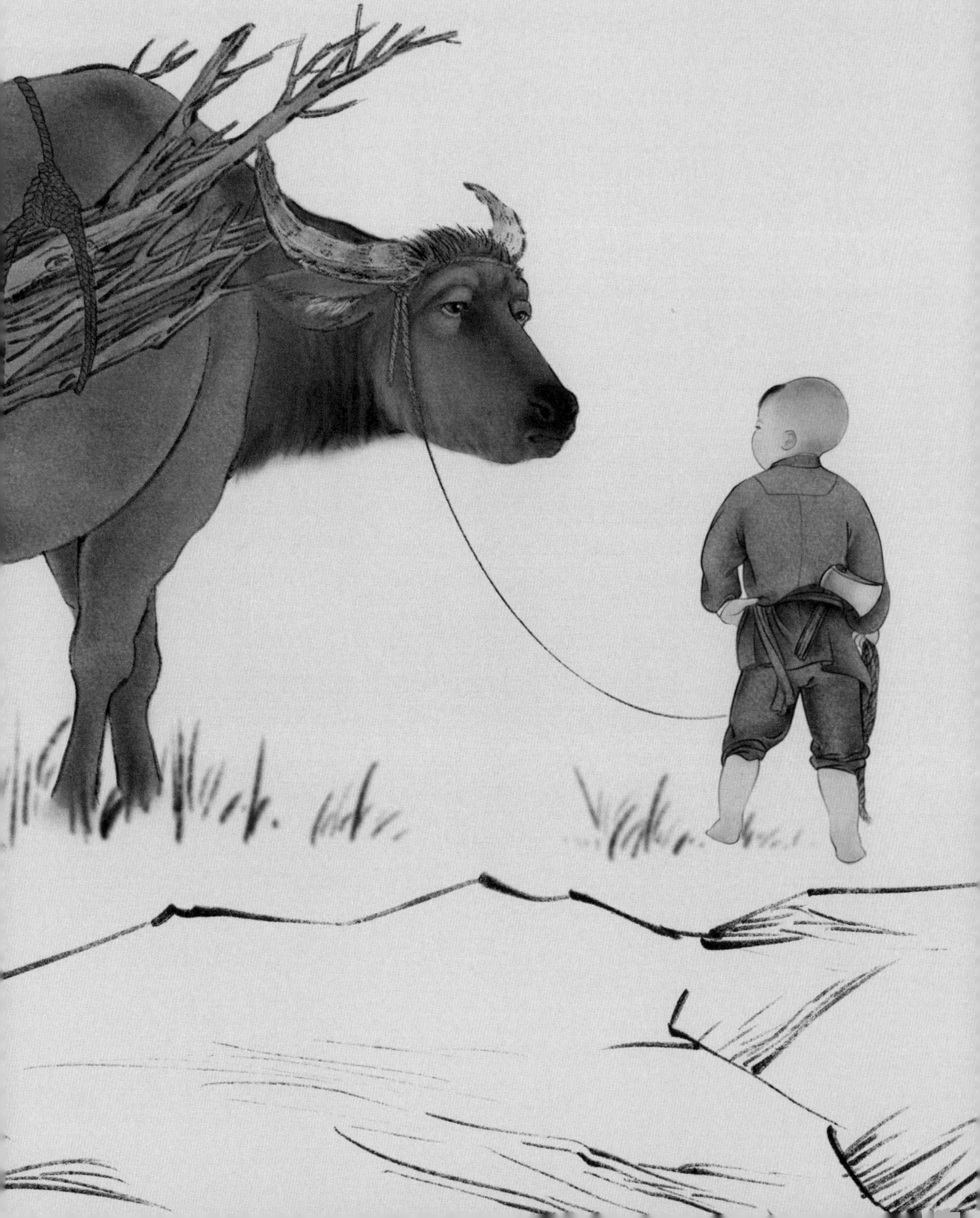

Sometimes you can
only do a small, small
thing for others.

And that can make
all the difference.

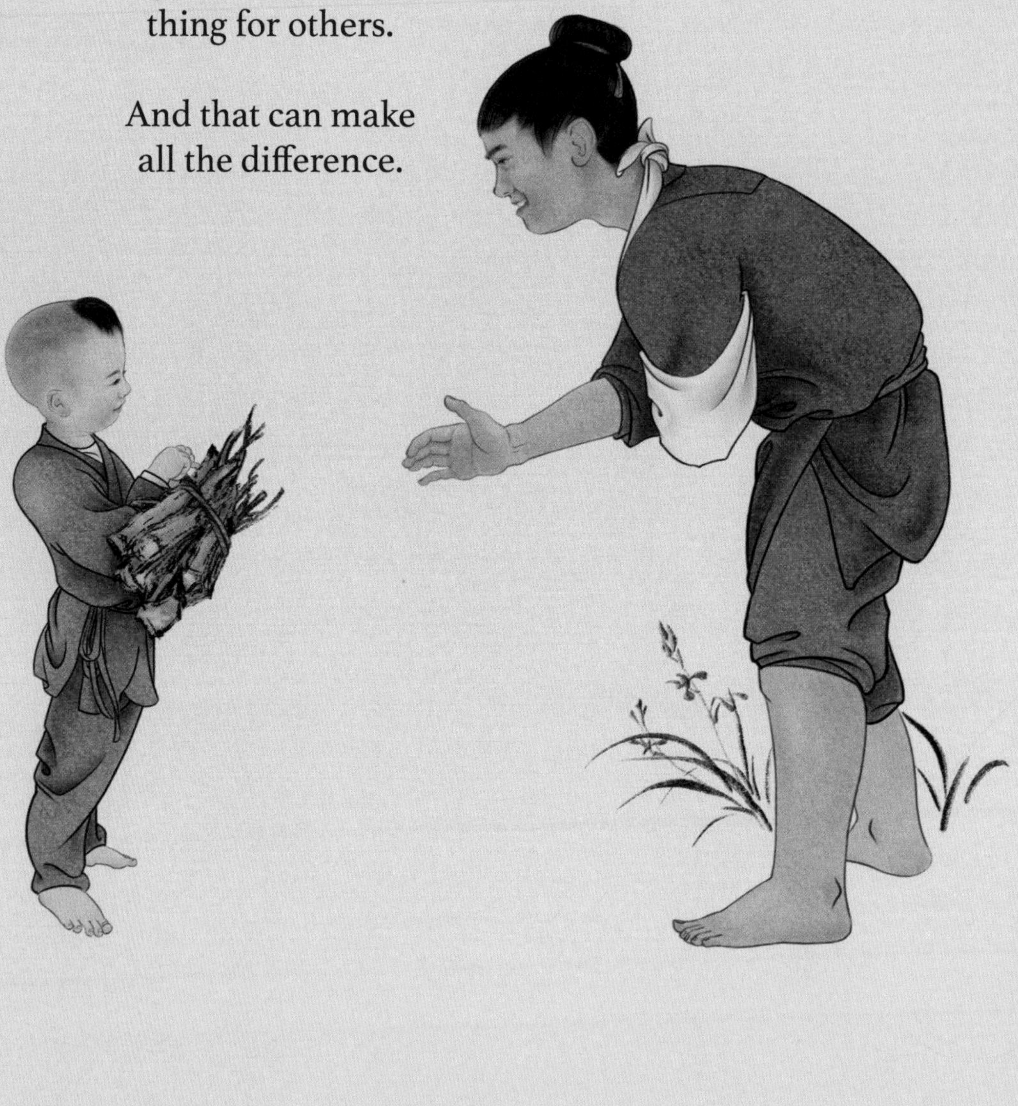

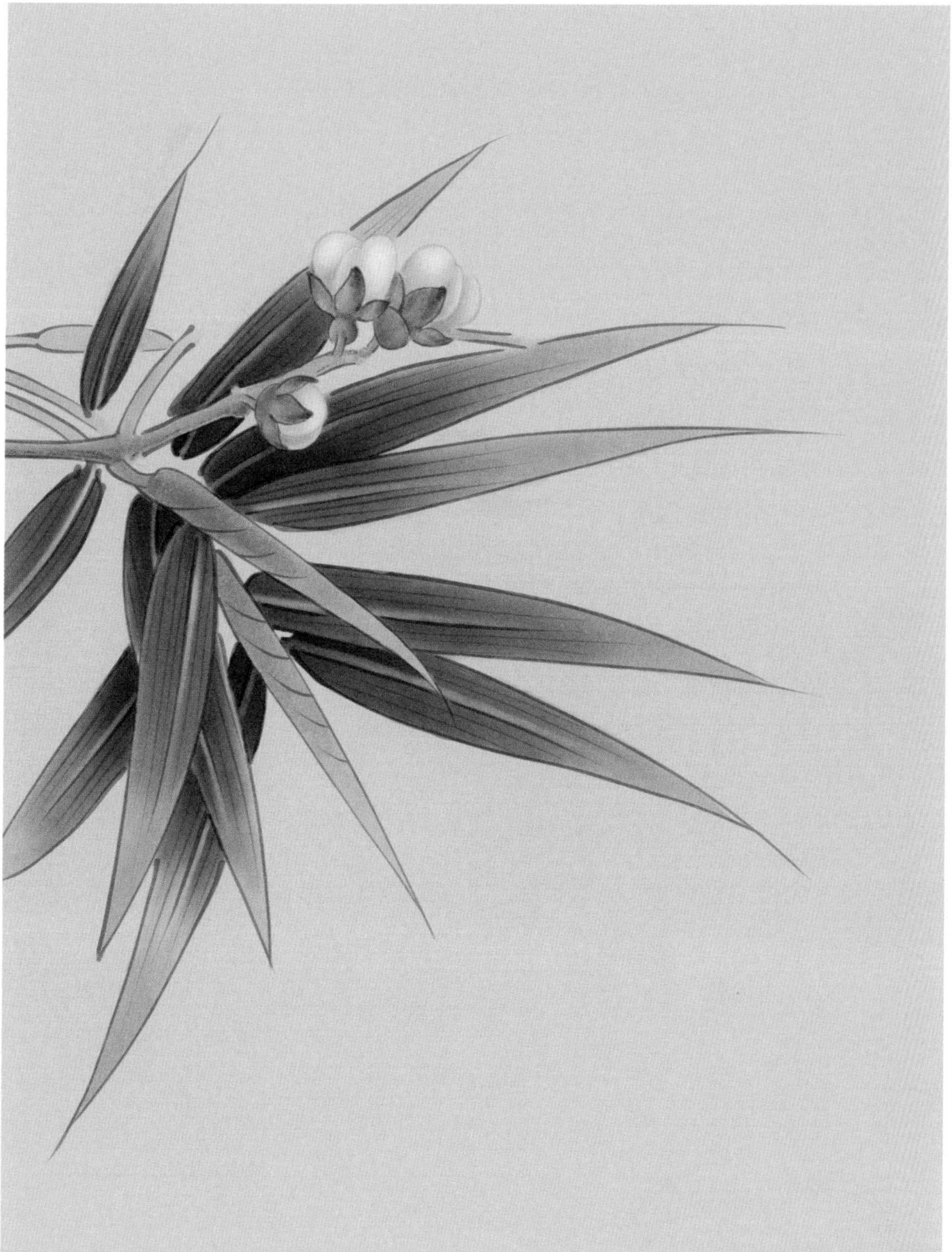

"After all is said and done," the oxherd boy said, "there really is nothing lovelier than an afternoon with nothing to do."

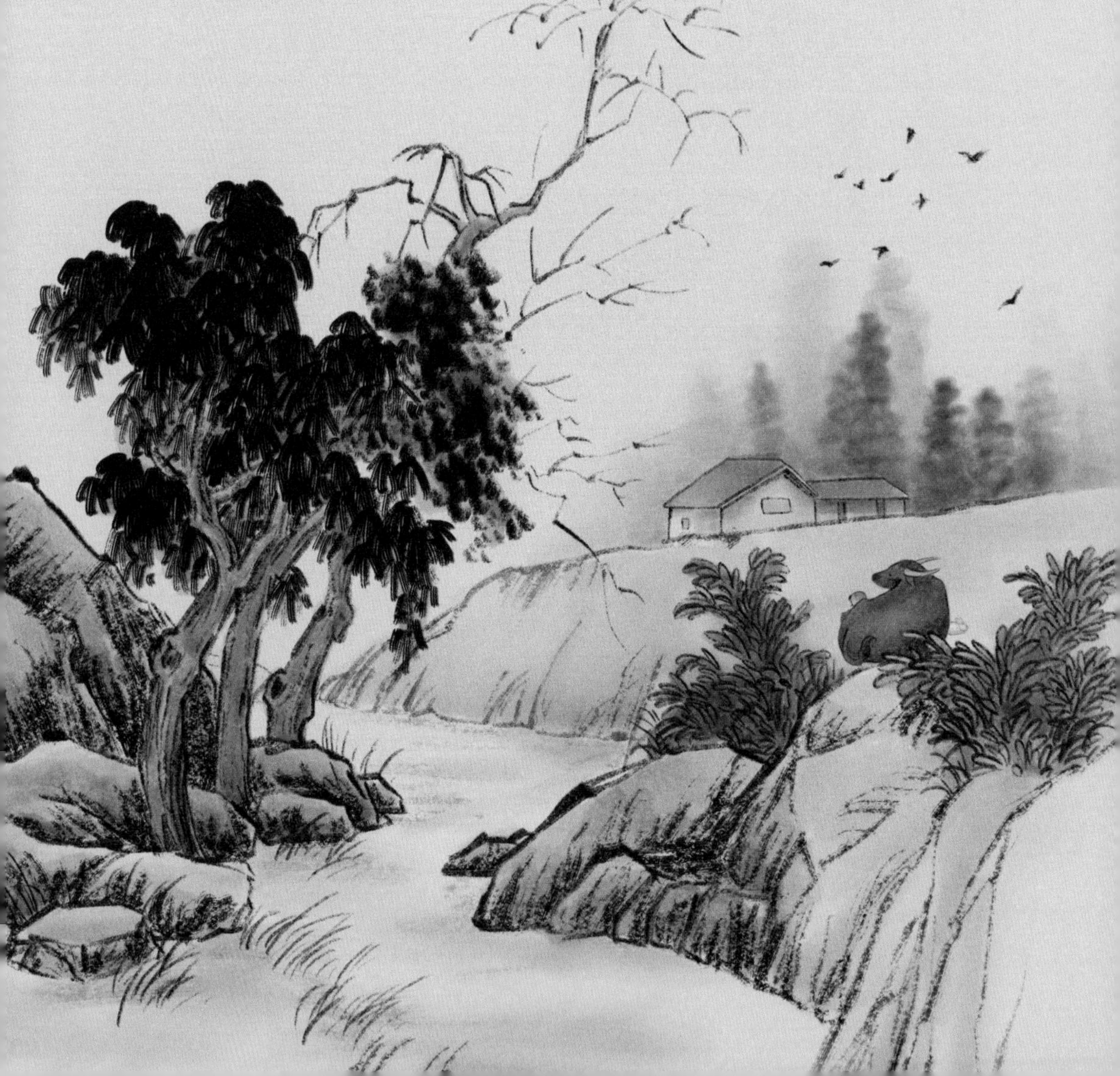

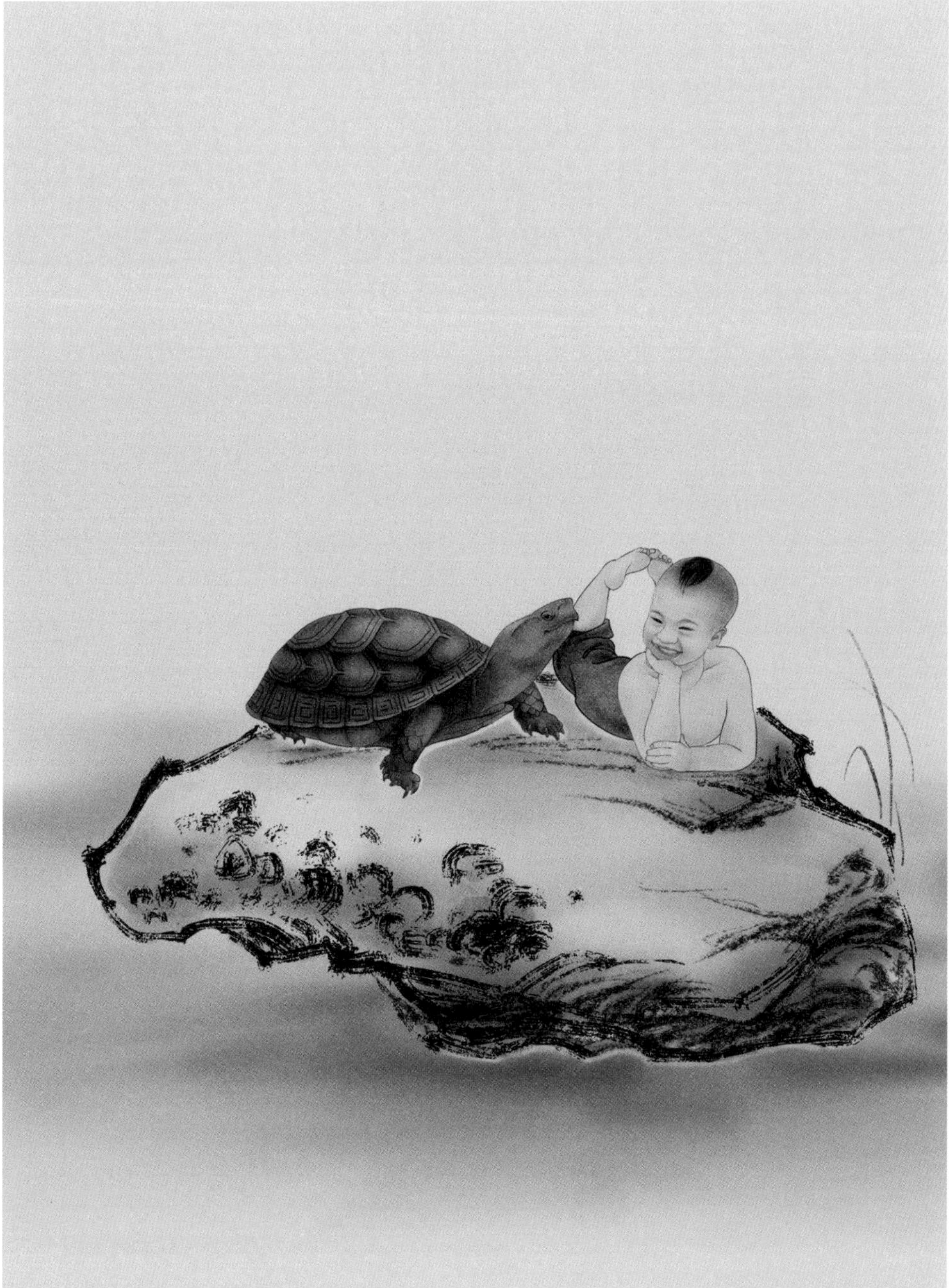

There was time for other things, too. One morning, the grandfather said, "Let's go for a walk."

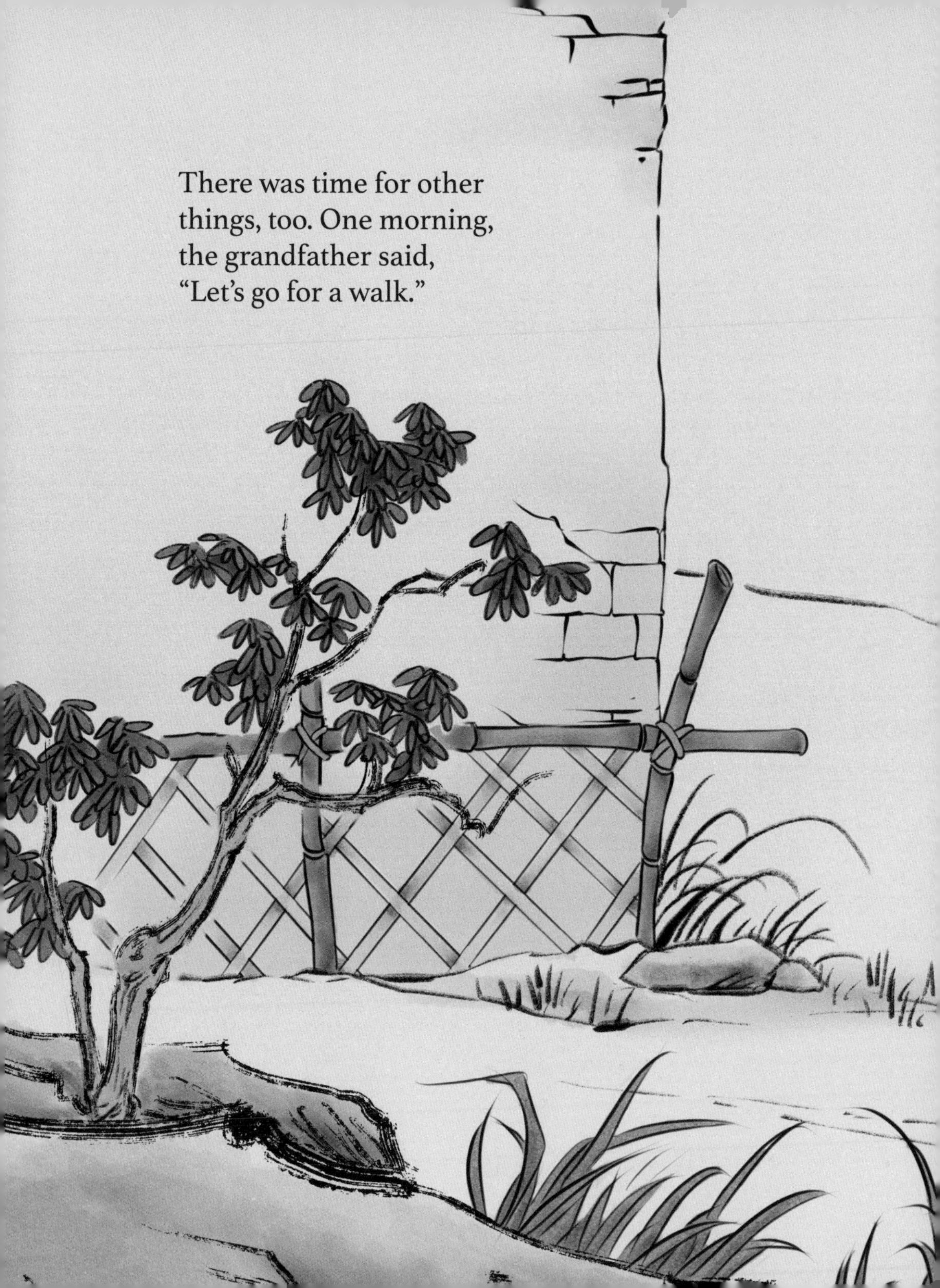

"Where are we going?"
asked the oxherd boy.

"Does it matter?"

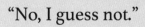

"No, I guess not."

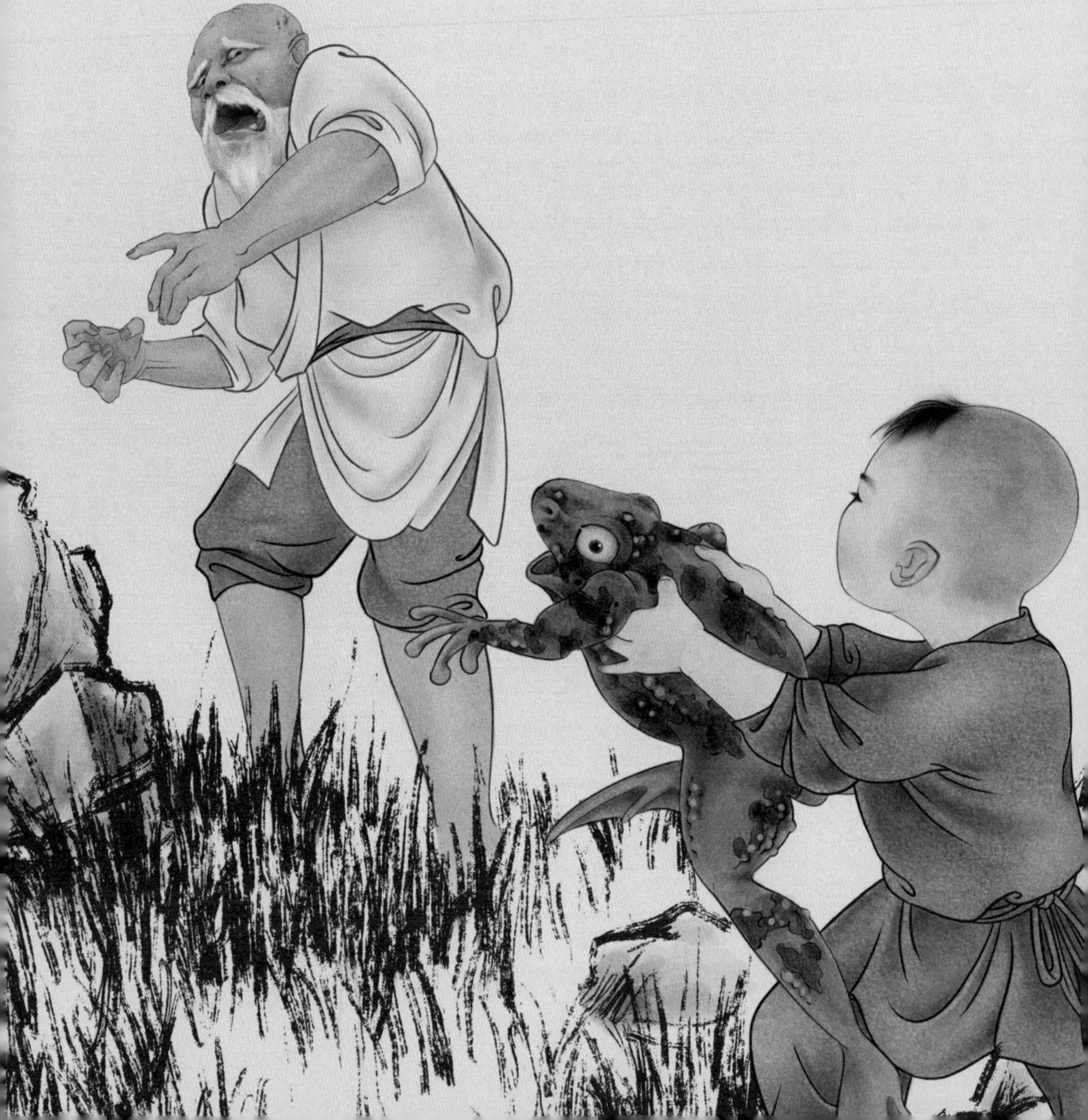

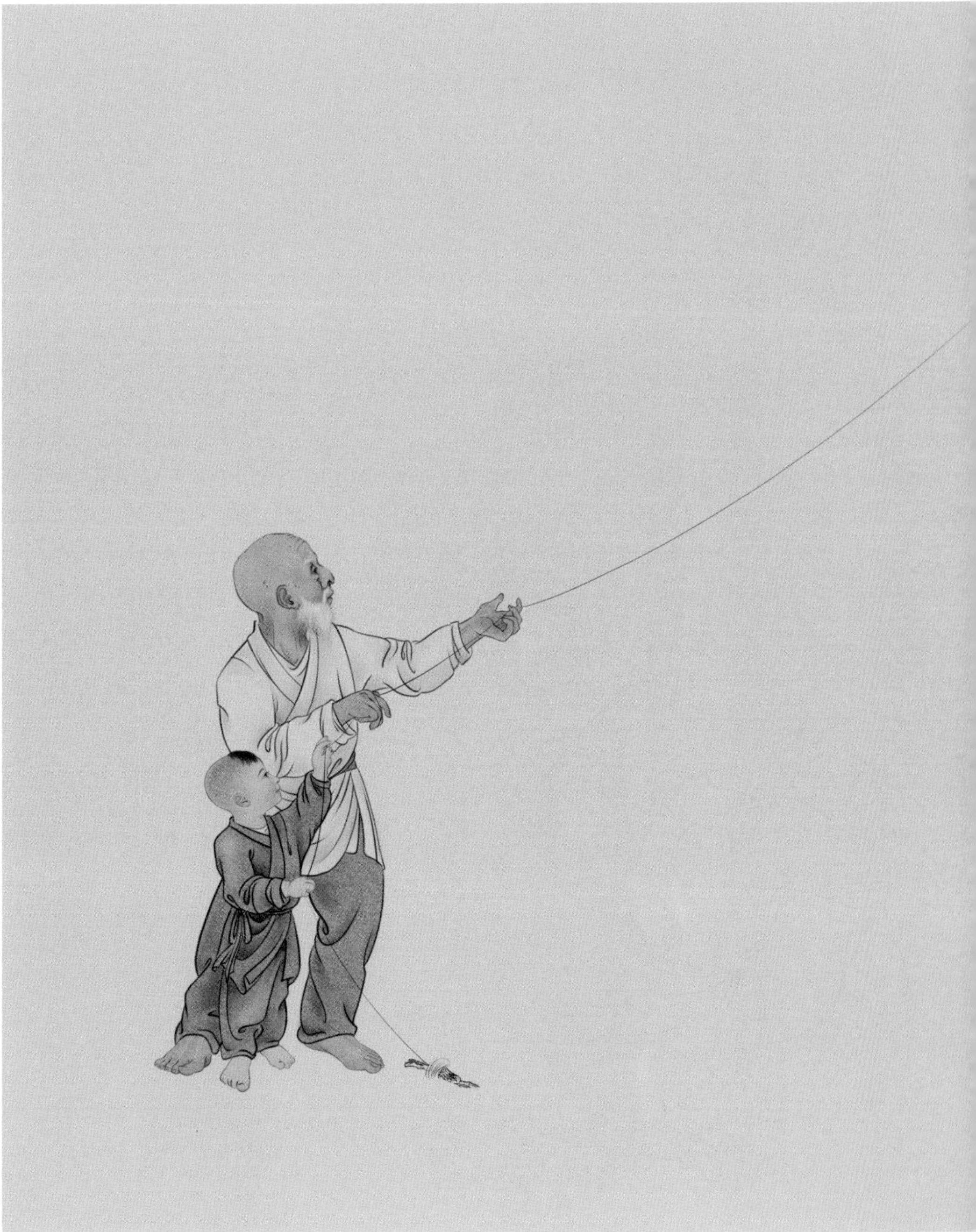

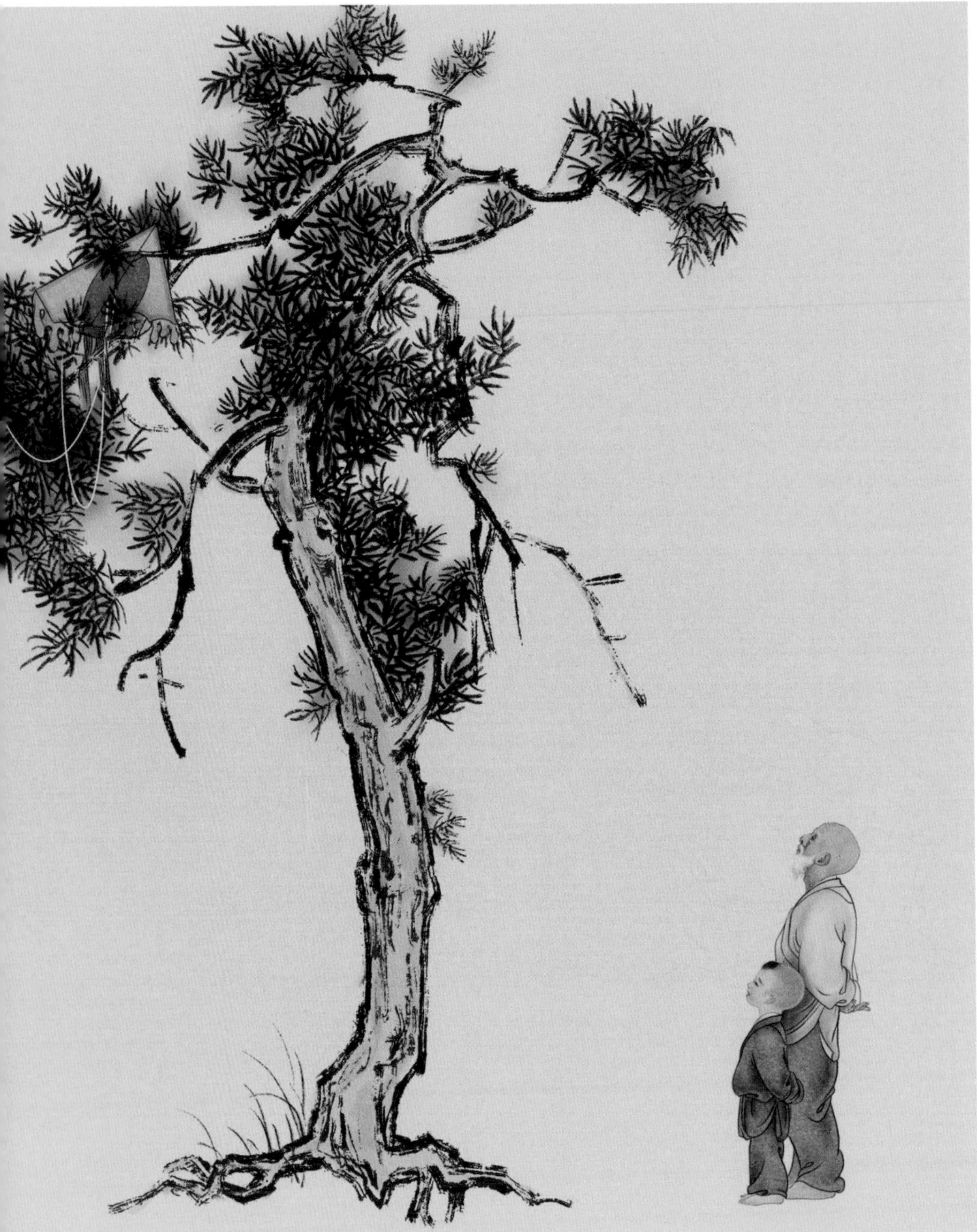

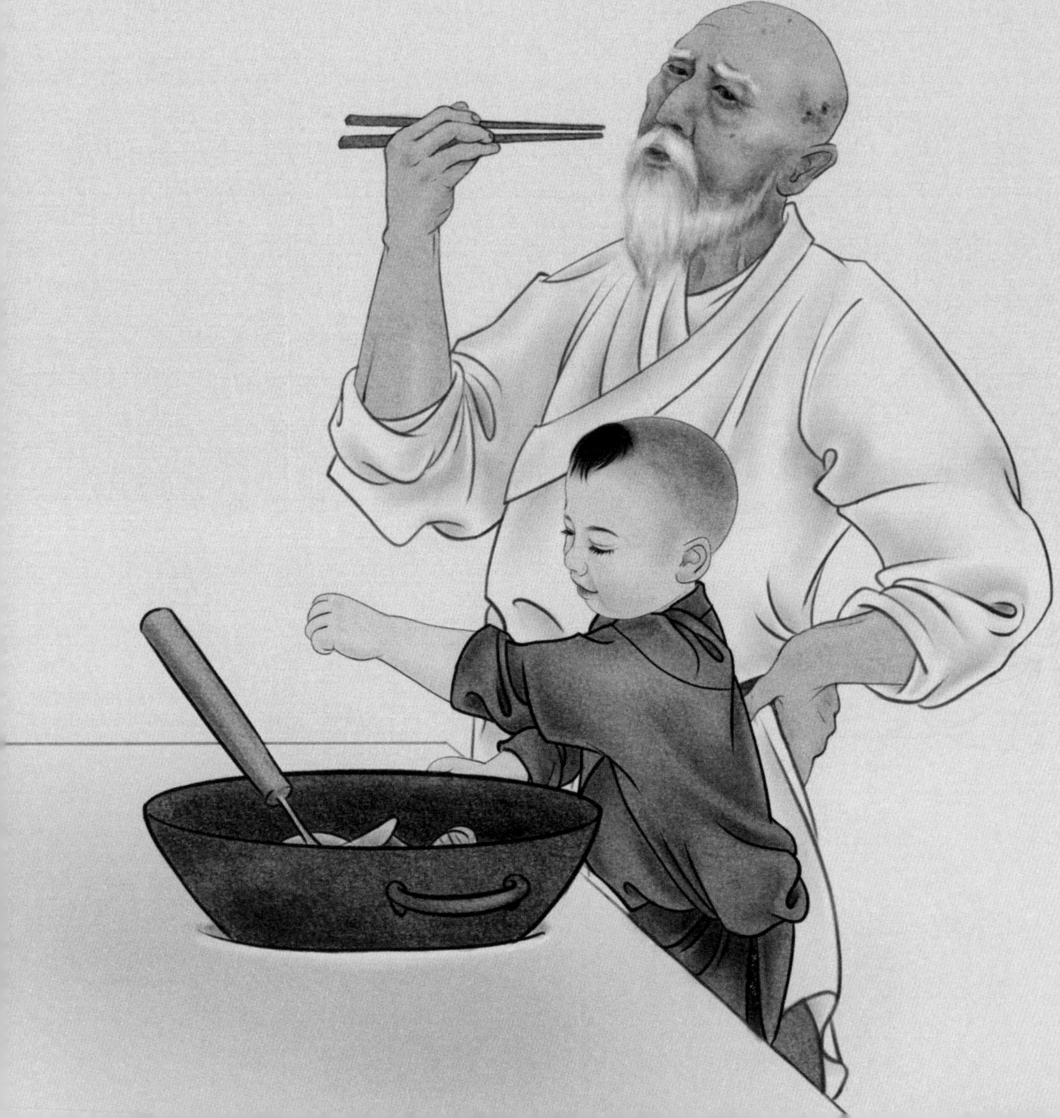

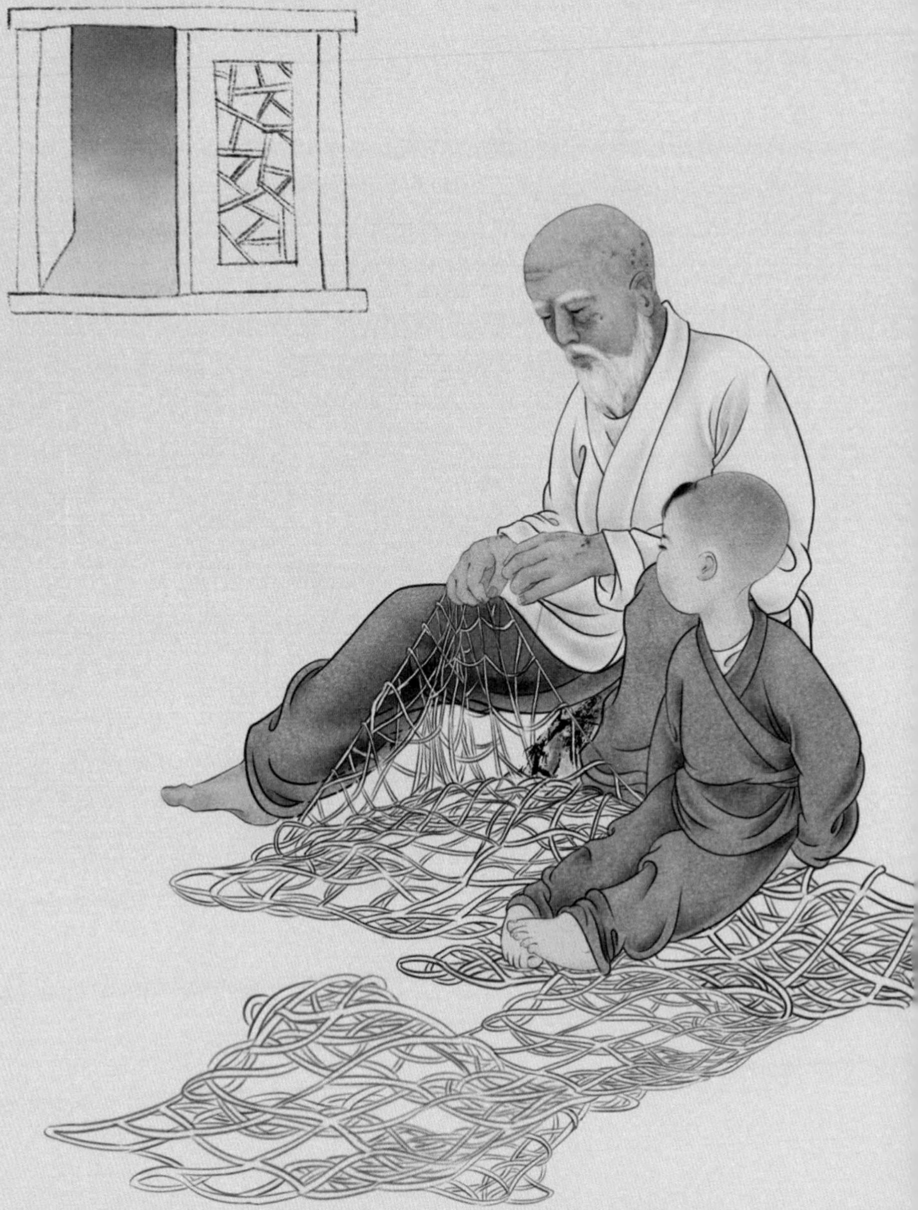

"Thank you," murmured the boy as he fell asleep.

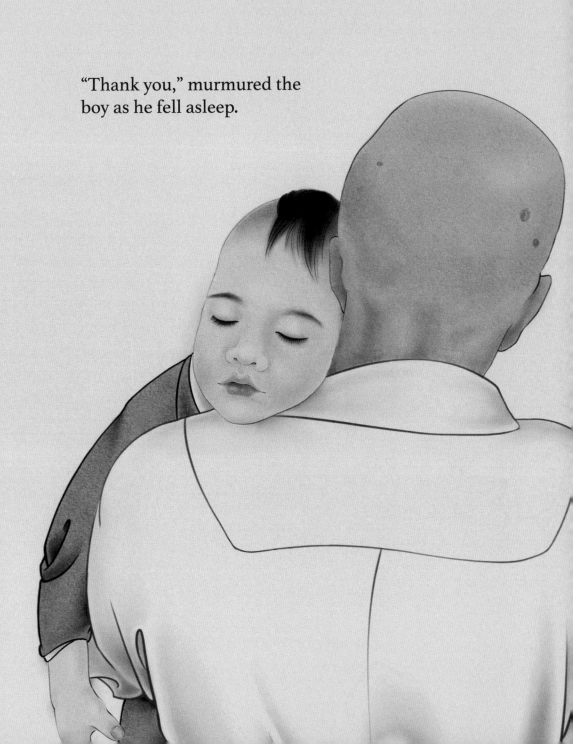

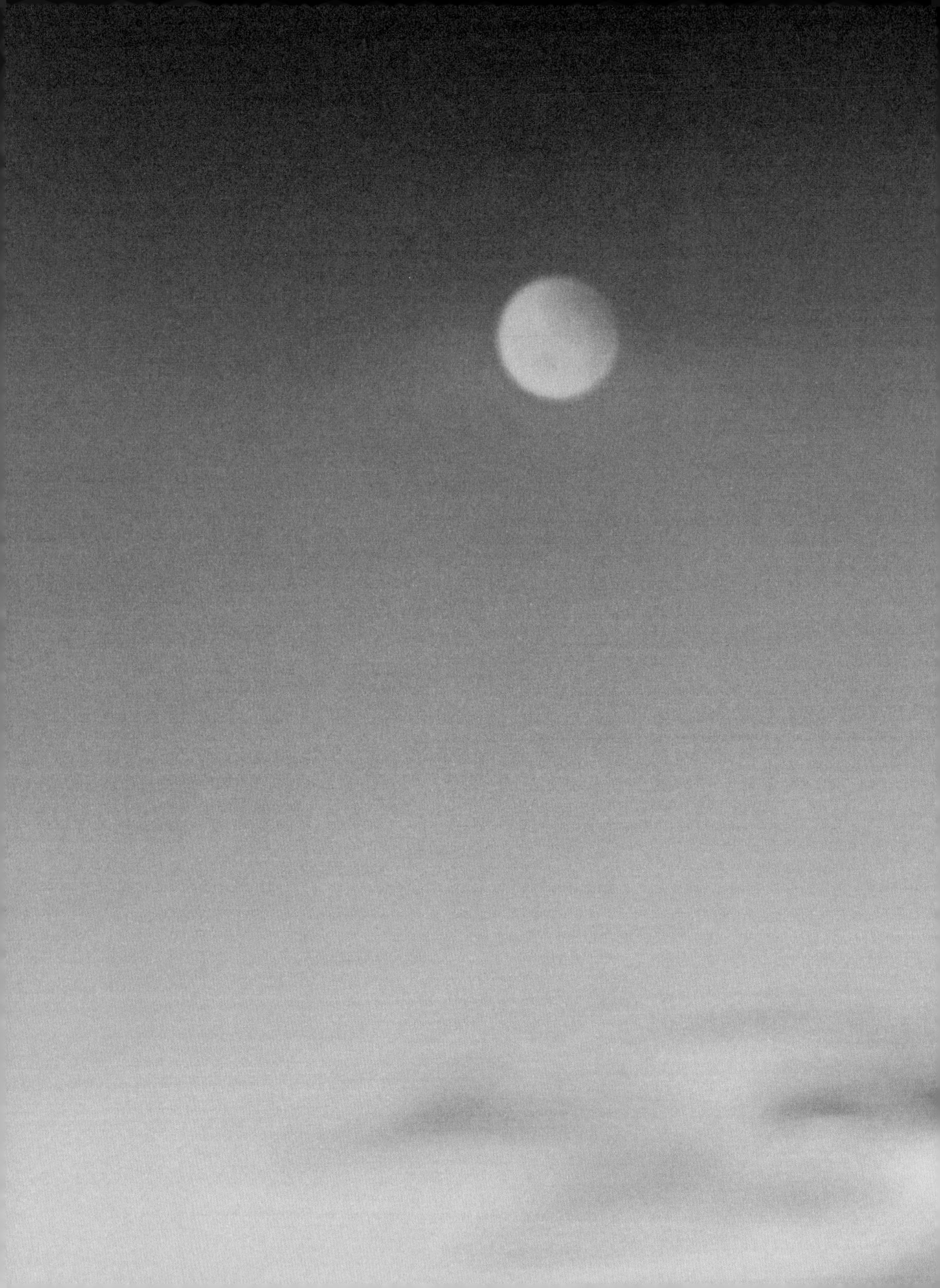

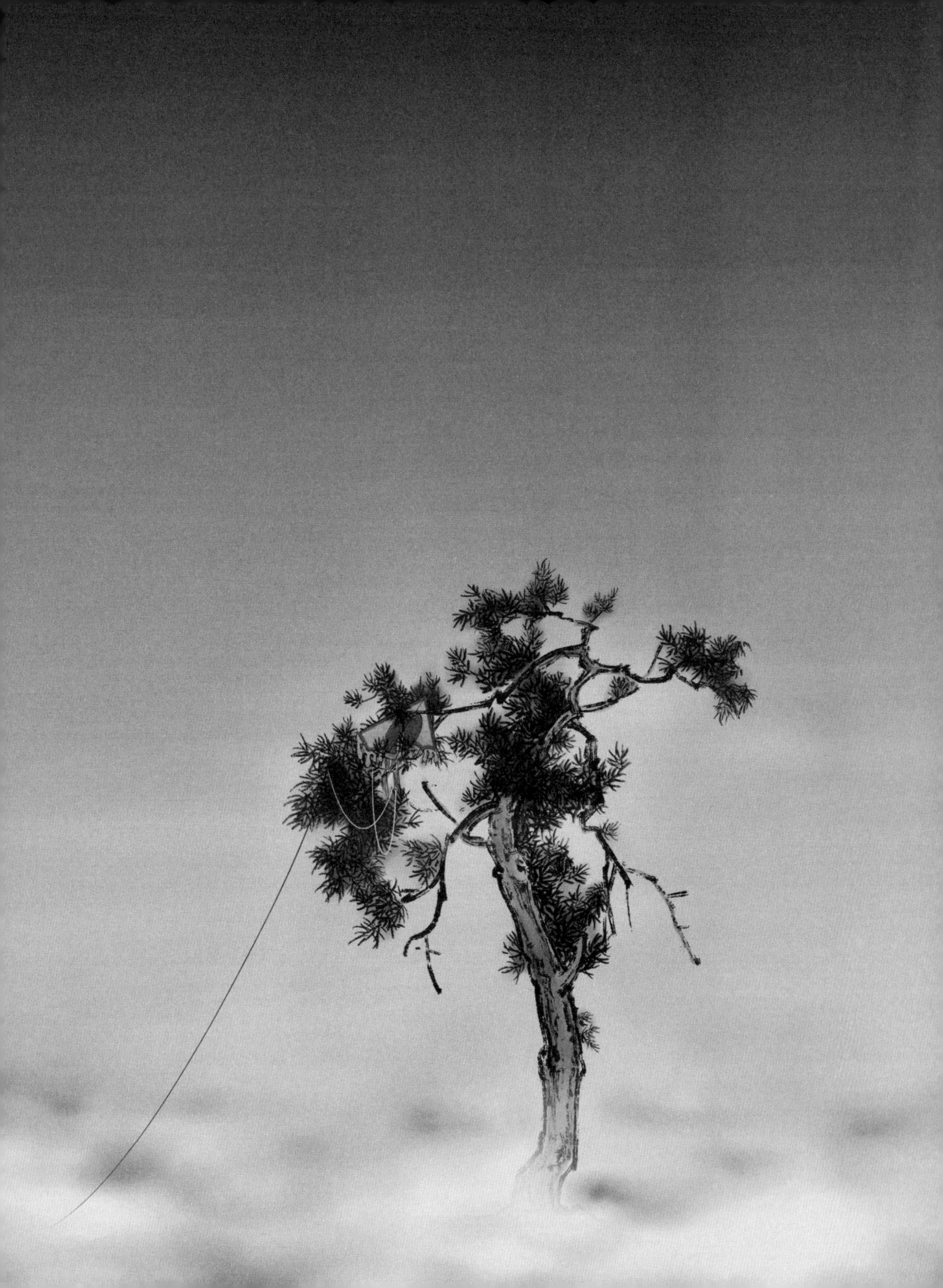

There were even worlds beyond
what they saw every day.

"I had such a strange dream,
and yet it felt so real," said the
ox with a shake of his head.

"Well, who's to say it wasn't?"
the boy asked.

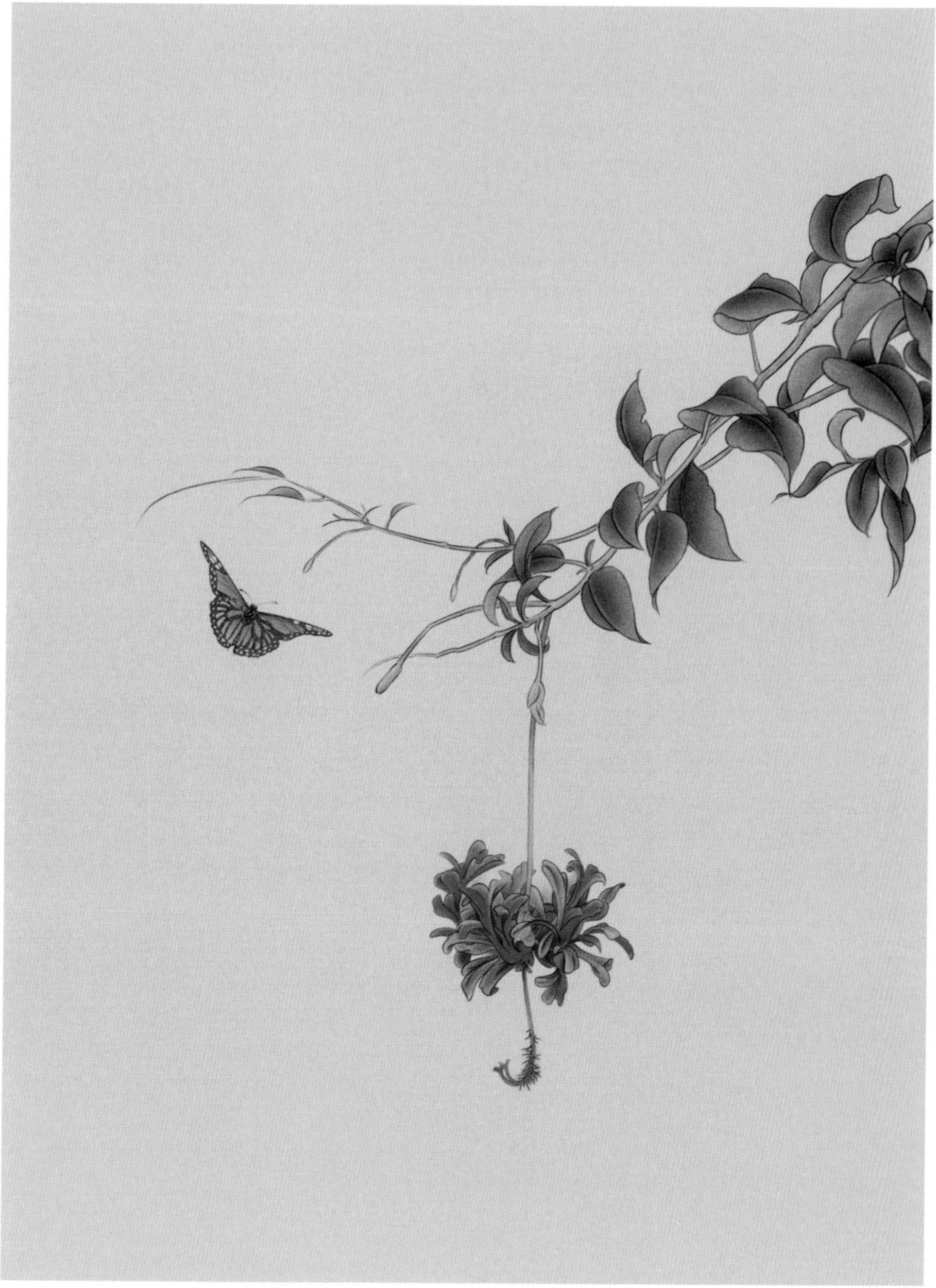

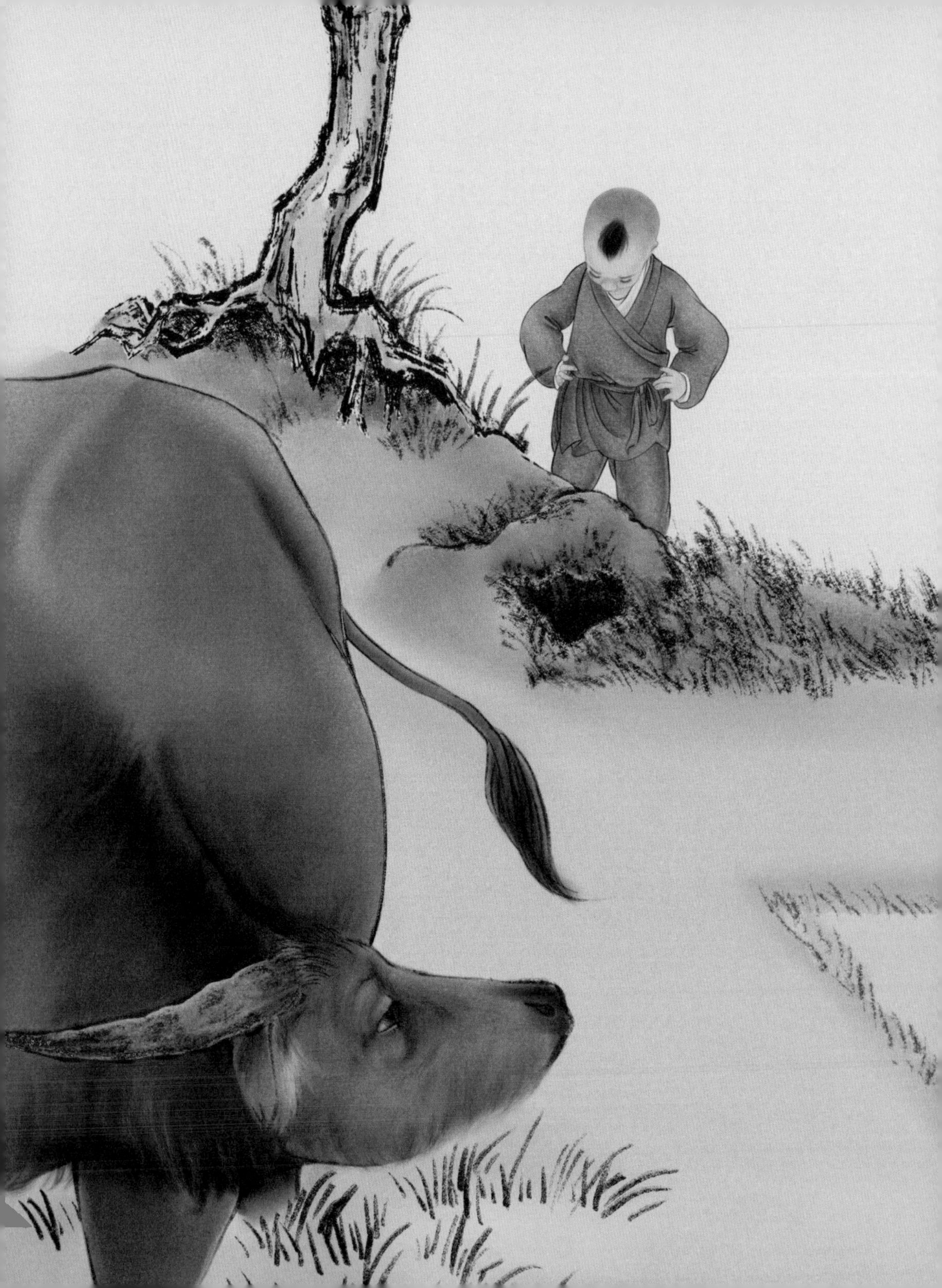

One morning, the oxherd boy noticed a cabbage had gone missing from the garden. “What do you think is down there?” he wondered.

“Maybe a new friend,” the ox suggested, “should we so choose.”

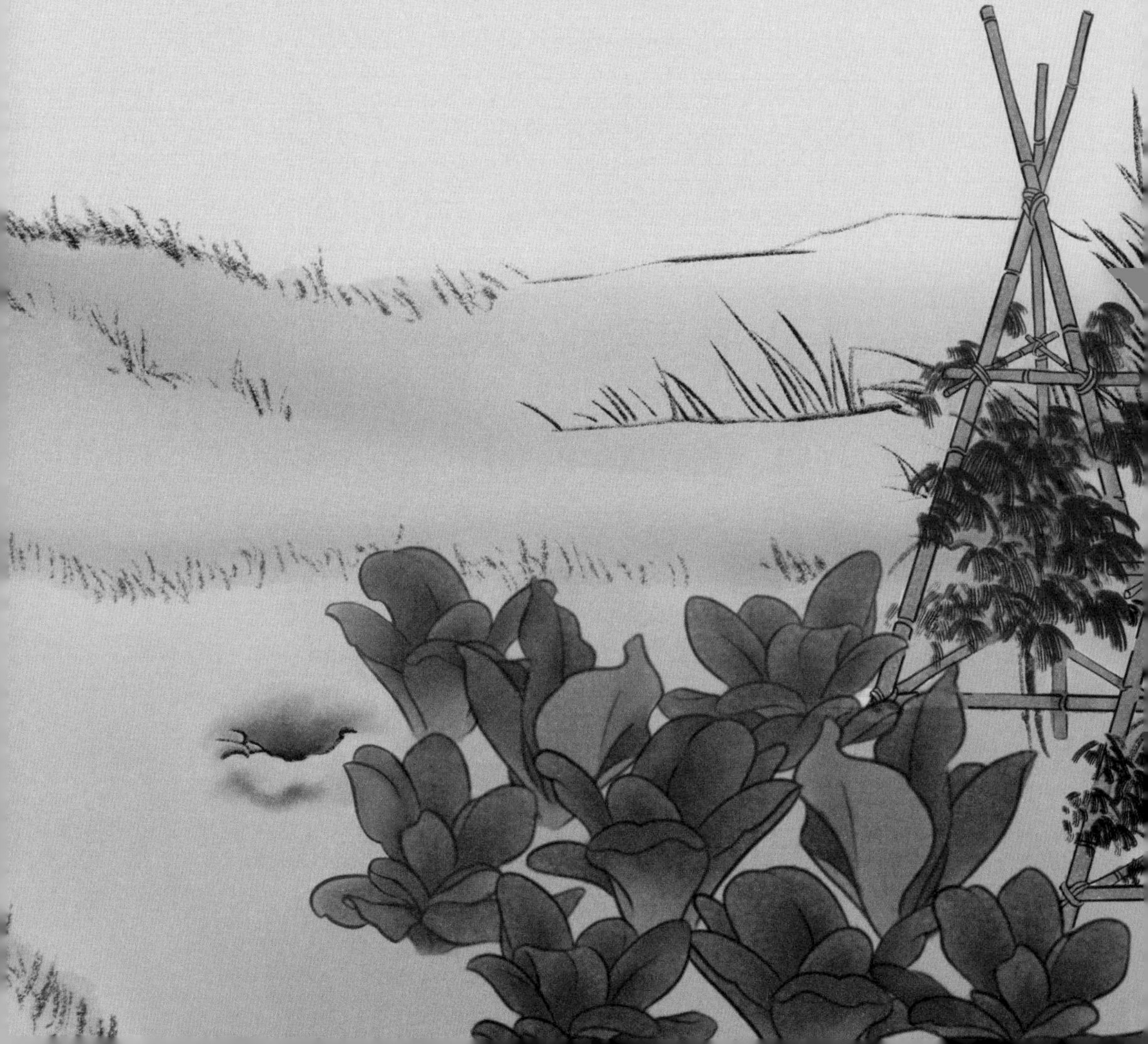

The rabbit's nose quivered
with curiosity. "Who are
you?" she asked.

The oxherd boy drew closer.
"I guess I'm just another you,
only different."

Isn't it strange how sometimes
we build up walls . . .

. . . only to wonder at the beauty
of letting someone in?

"Thank you," said the rabbit.

Sometimes you can
only do a small,
small thing.

And that can make
all the difference.

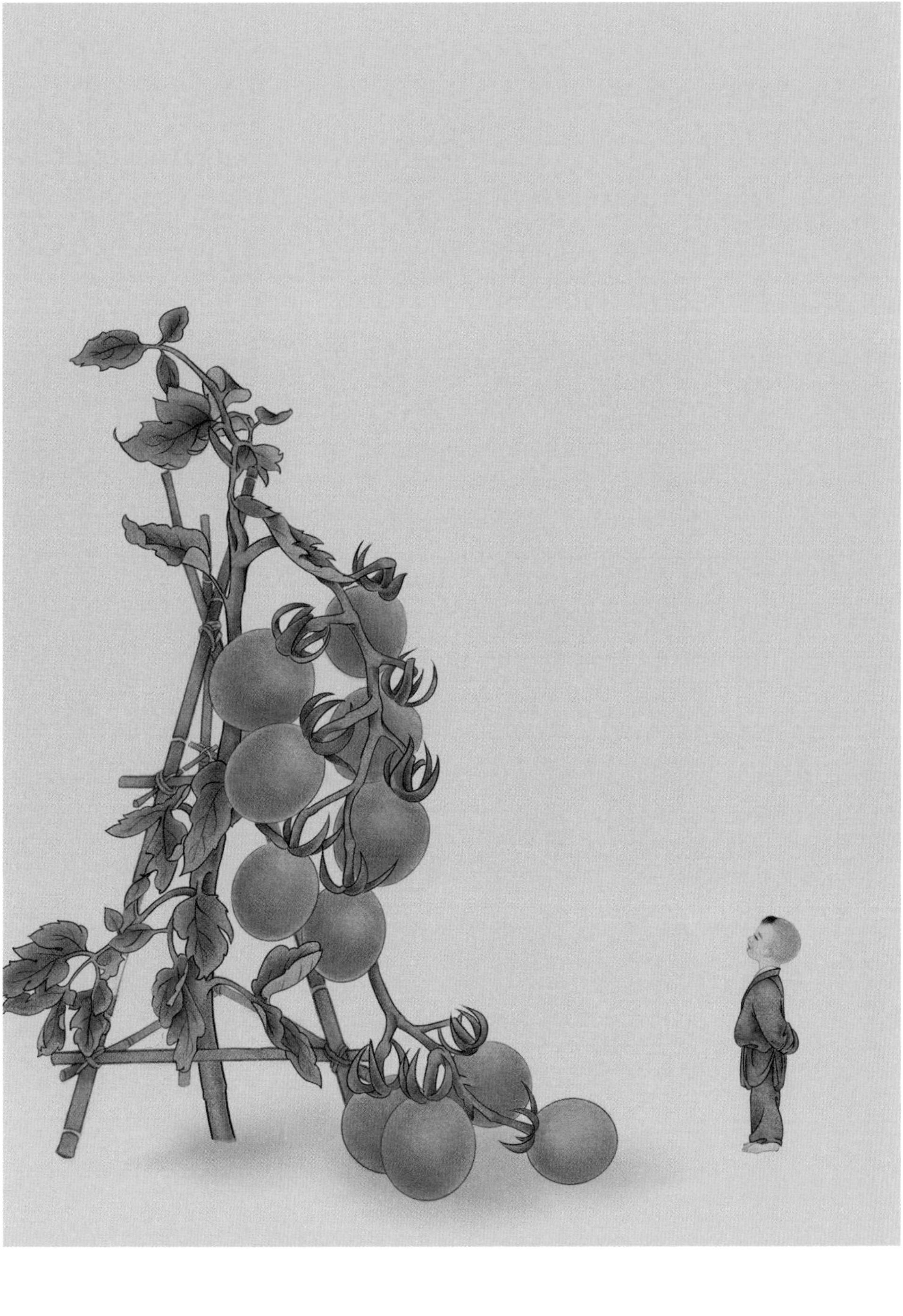

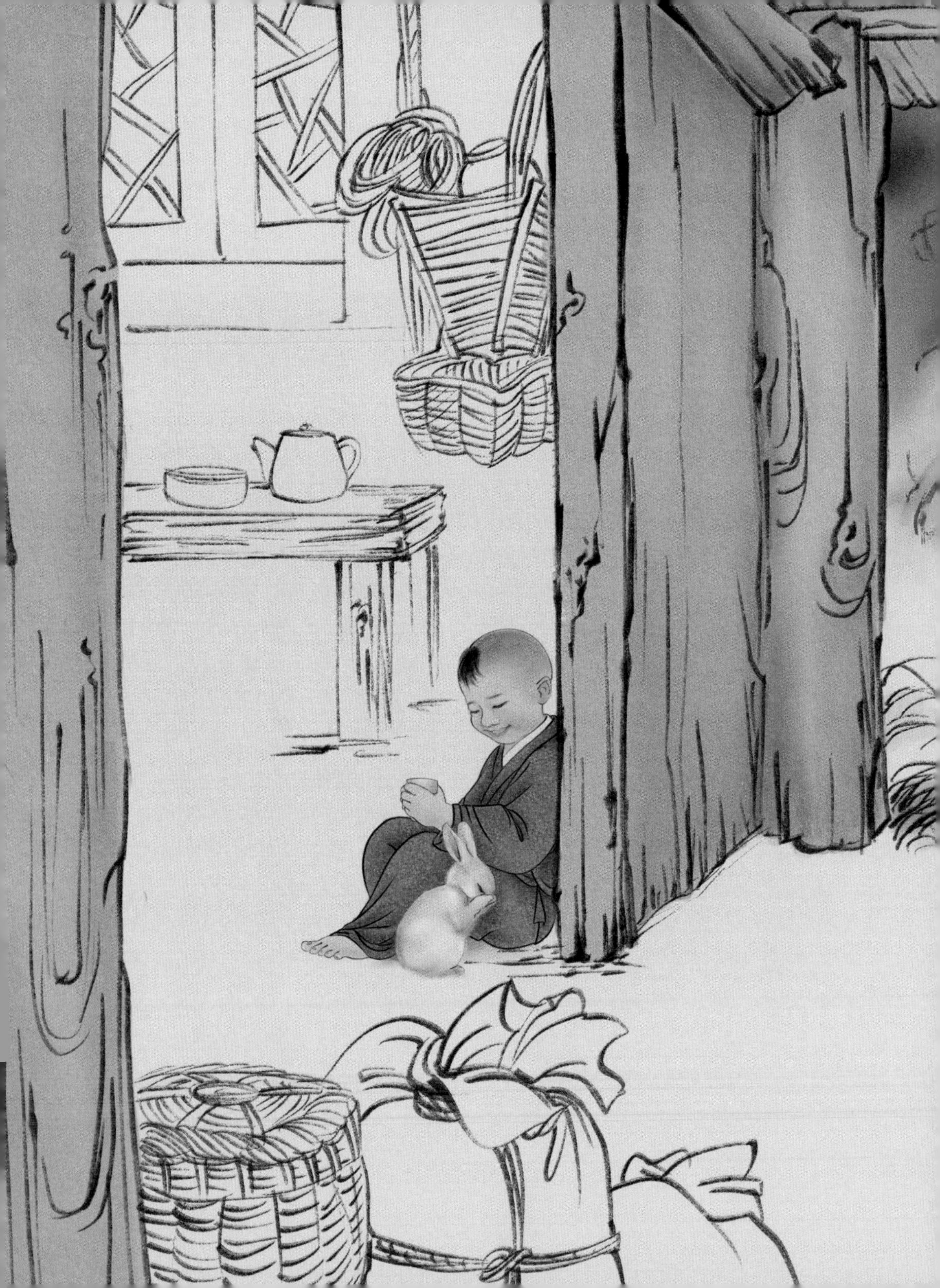

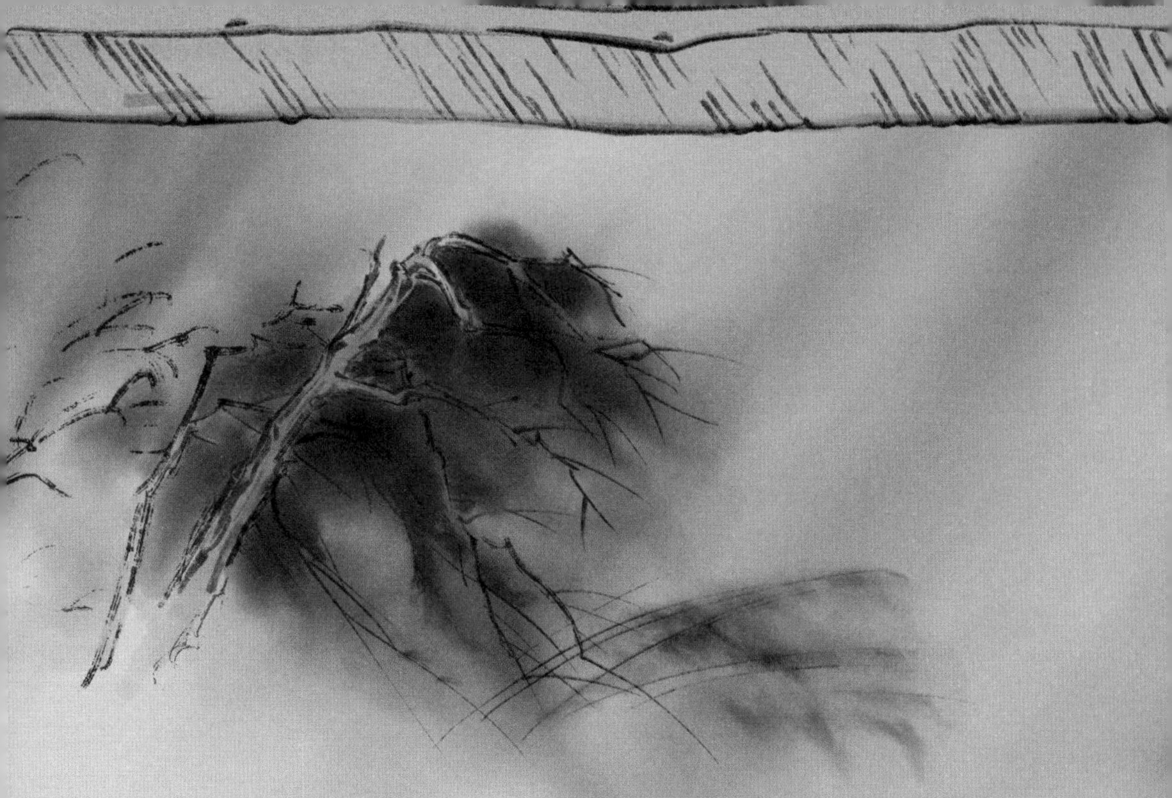

A storm visited now and then.
"What a terrible day!" the rabbit said.

"That gave us this cozy afternoon at home," concluded the boy.

"Have you noticed that the
grass is all that remains
standing after the storm?"
marveled the ox.

The oxherd boy nodded.
"Sometimes soft can be strong."

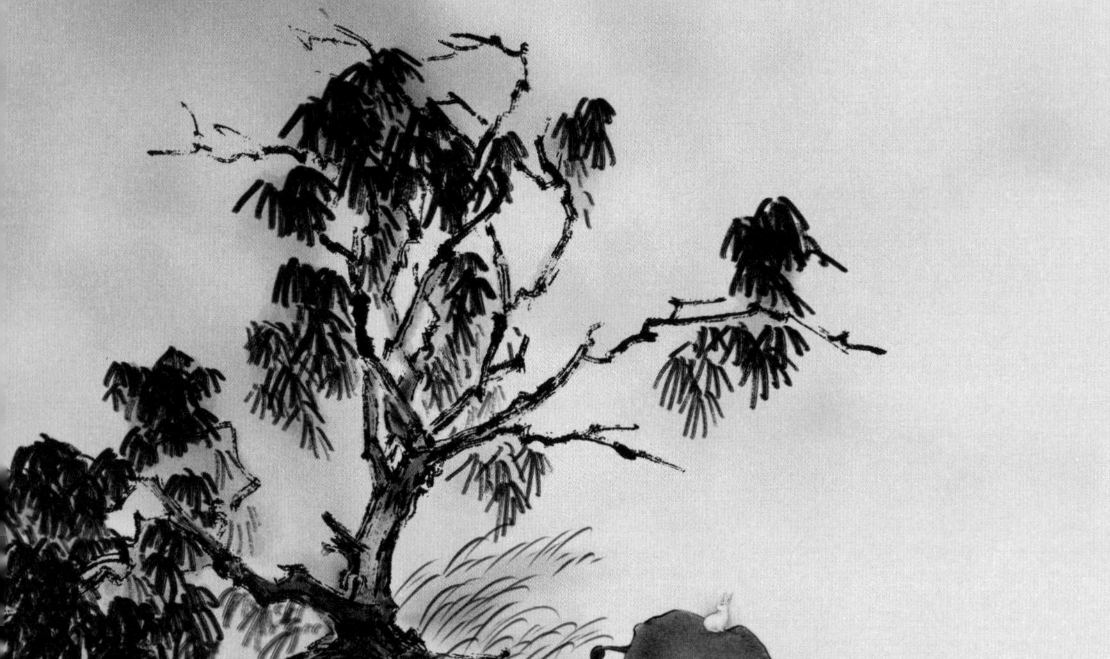

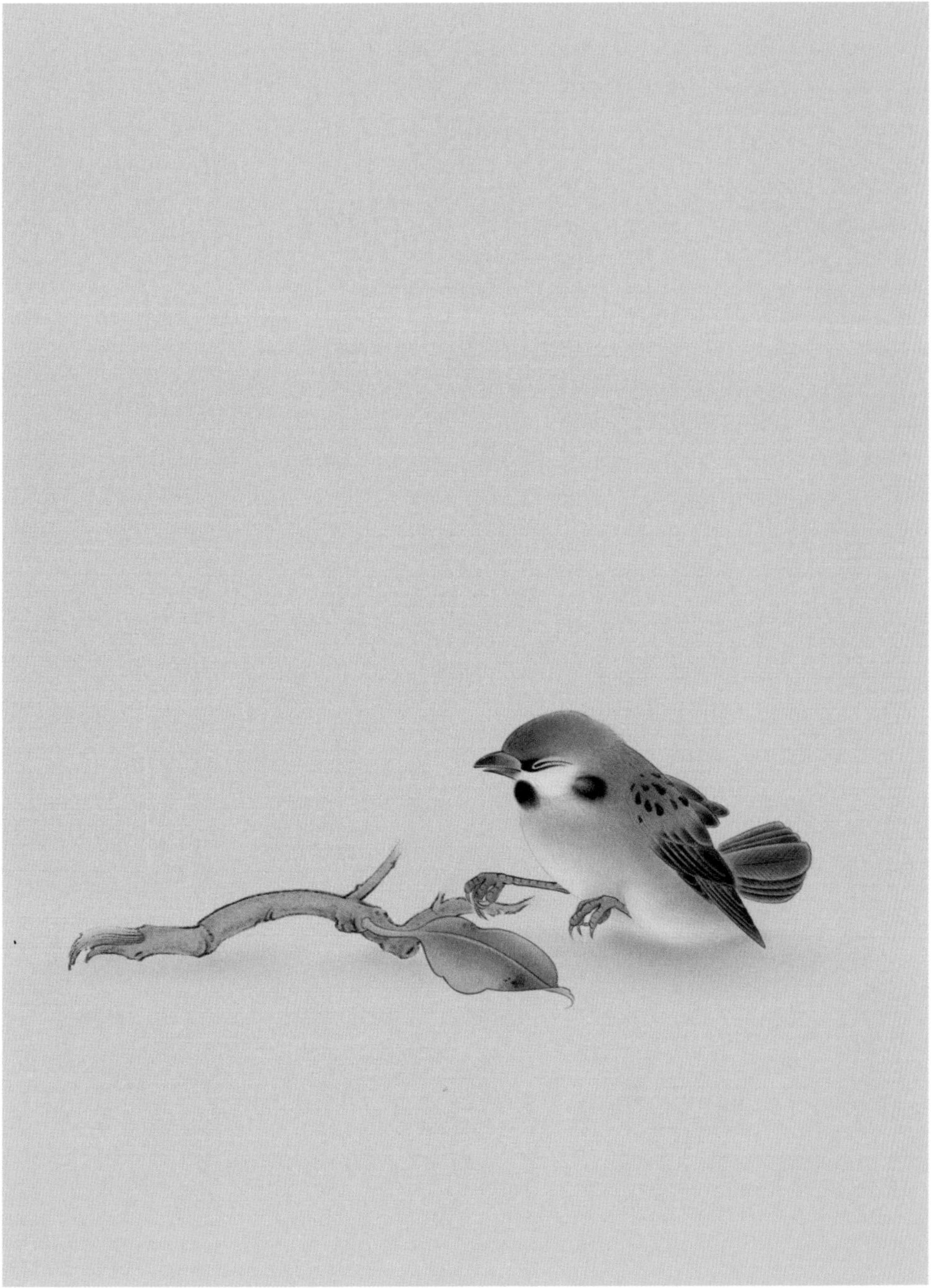

Little by little, the sparrow grew
stronger. "We'll take care of
him until he's ready to fly," said
the boy.

The rabbit began to worry.
"But then he might leave us."

"Isn't that the point?"

"It's nice the cage will always keep
me safe from falling," the sparrow said.

The oxherd boy shook his head.
"You're not safe because of the cage,
but because you have wings."

When the time came, the rabbit wiped her eyes. "I knew he would leave someday," she said, "so why does it still hurt?"

The oxherd boy wrapped her in his arms and nodded.

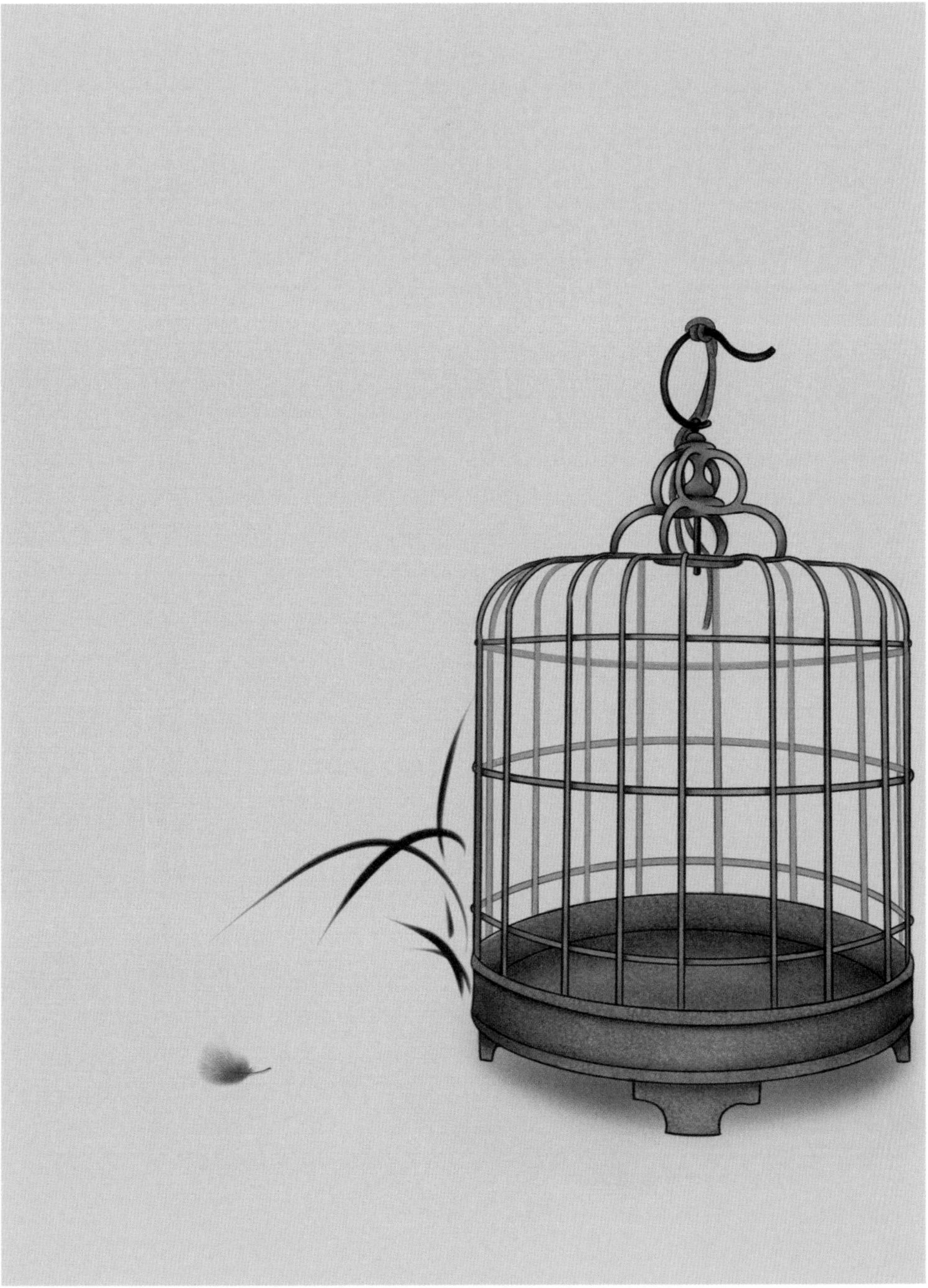

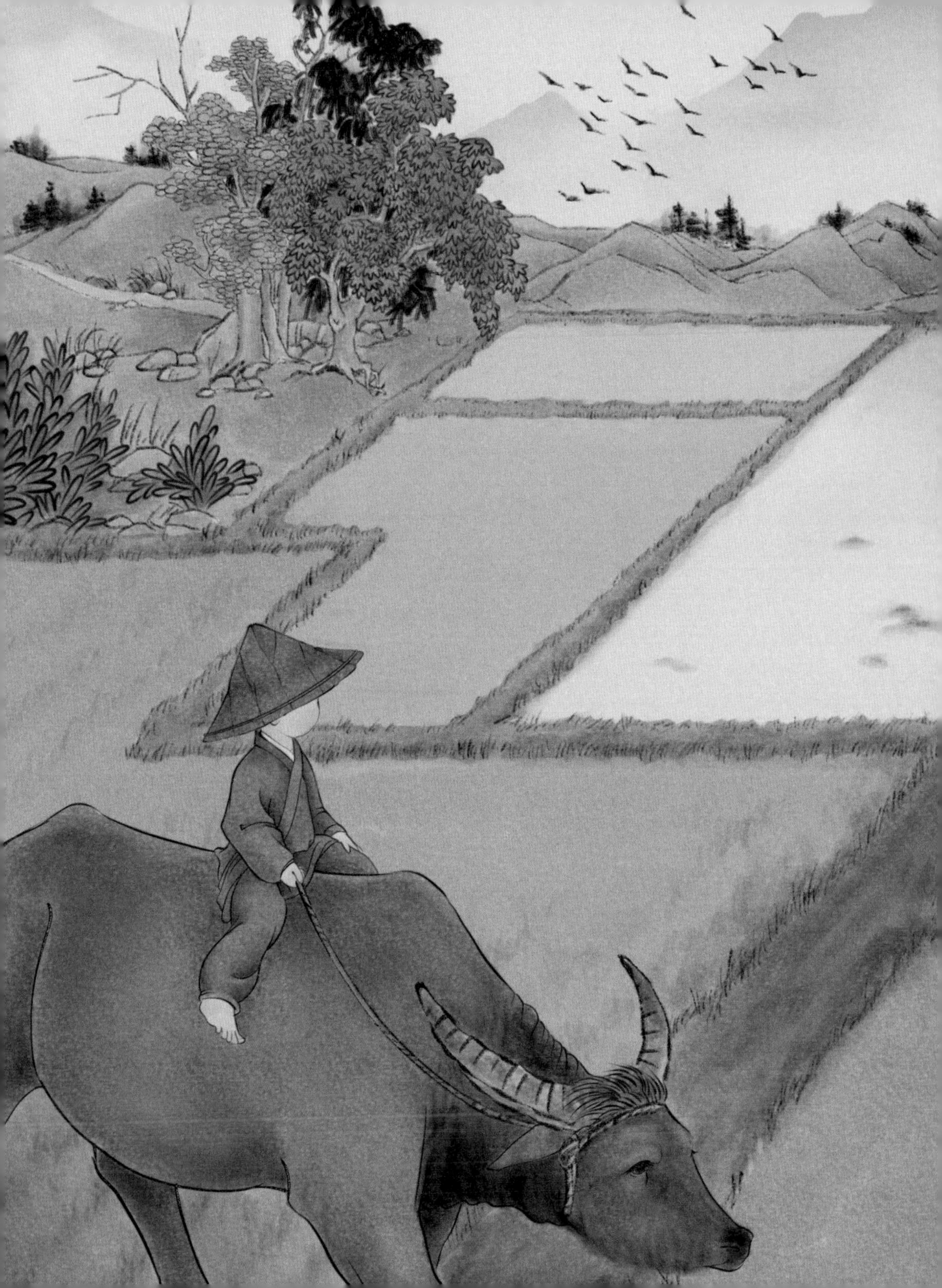

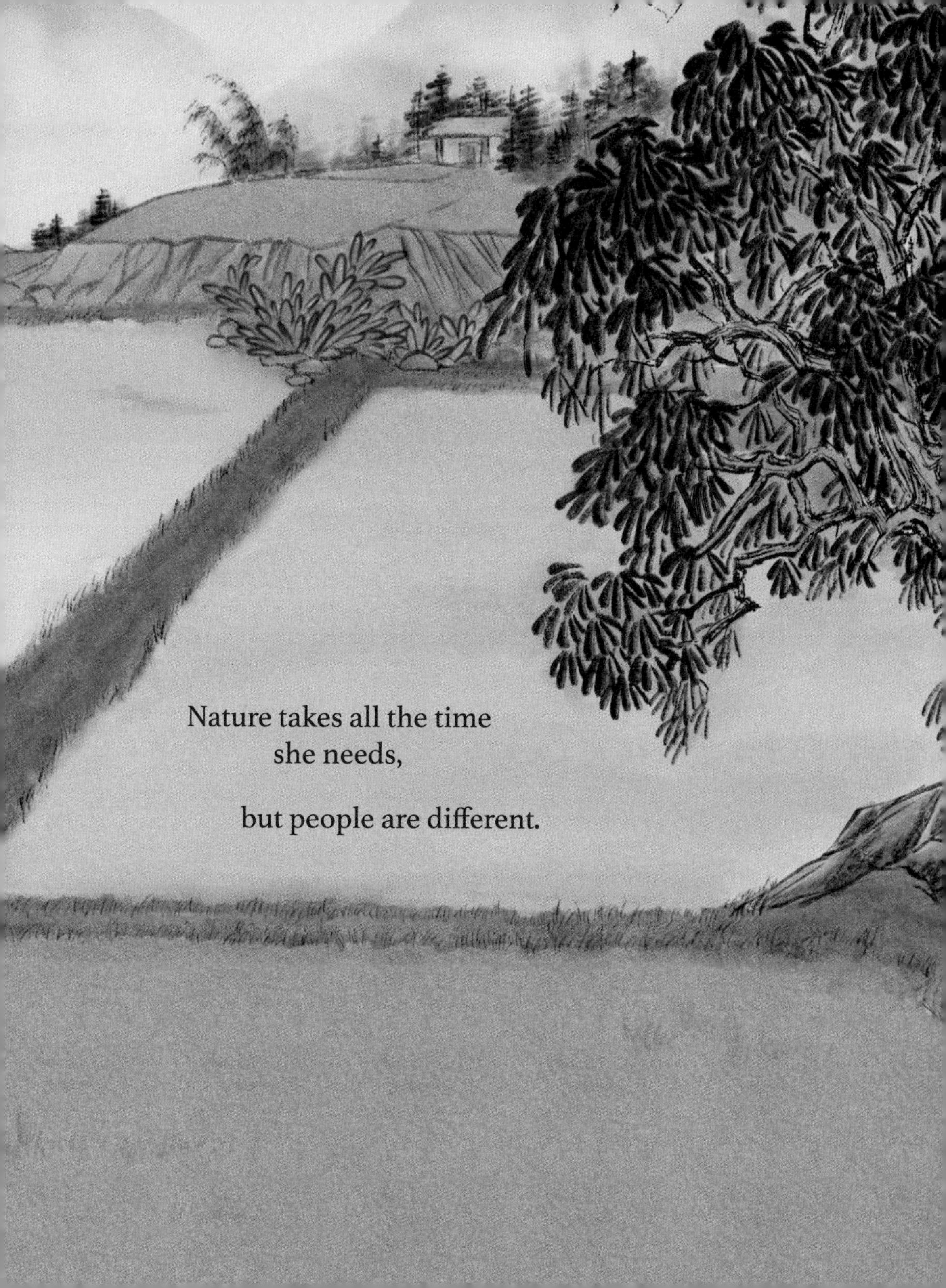

Nature takes all the time
she needs,

but people are different.

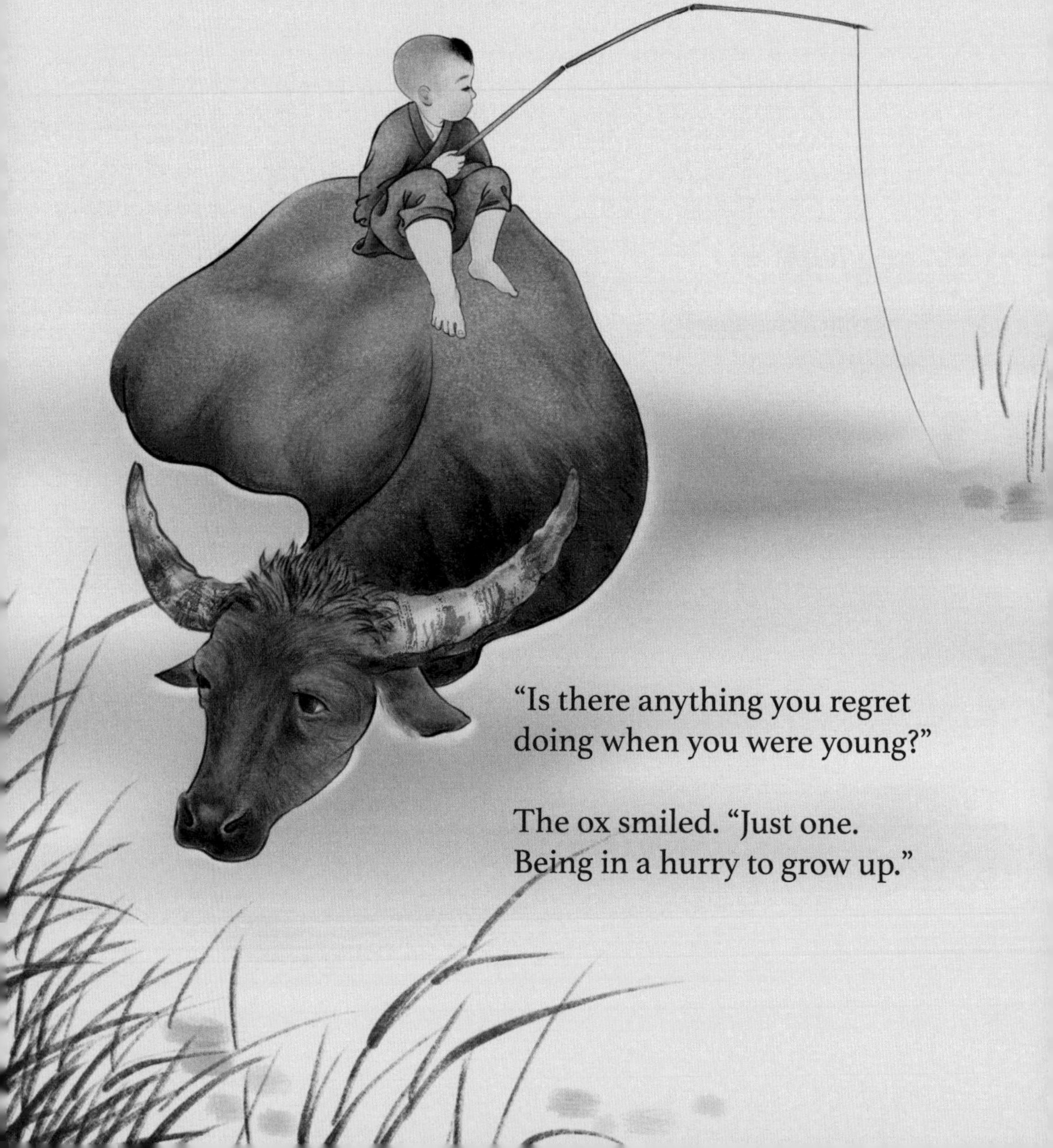

“Is there anything you regret doing when you were young?”

The ox smiled. “Just one. Being in a hurry to grow up.”

"Will you teach me everything
you know?" the oxherd boy asked.

"I don't think so," replied the ox,
"I'd rather relearn life with you
than simply pass on my old ways."

"Everyone says children are so lucky, that we live free because we have our whole lives ahead of us," the boy noted to his friends.

The ox thought for a moment before saying,

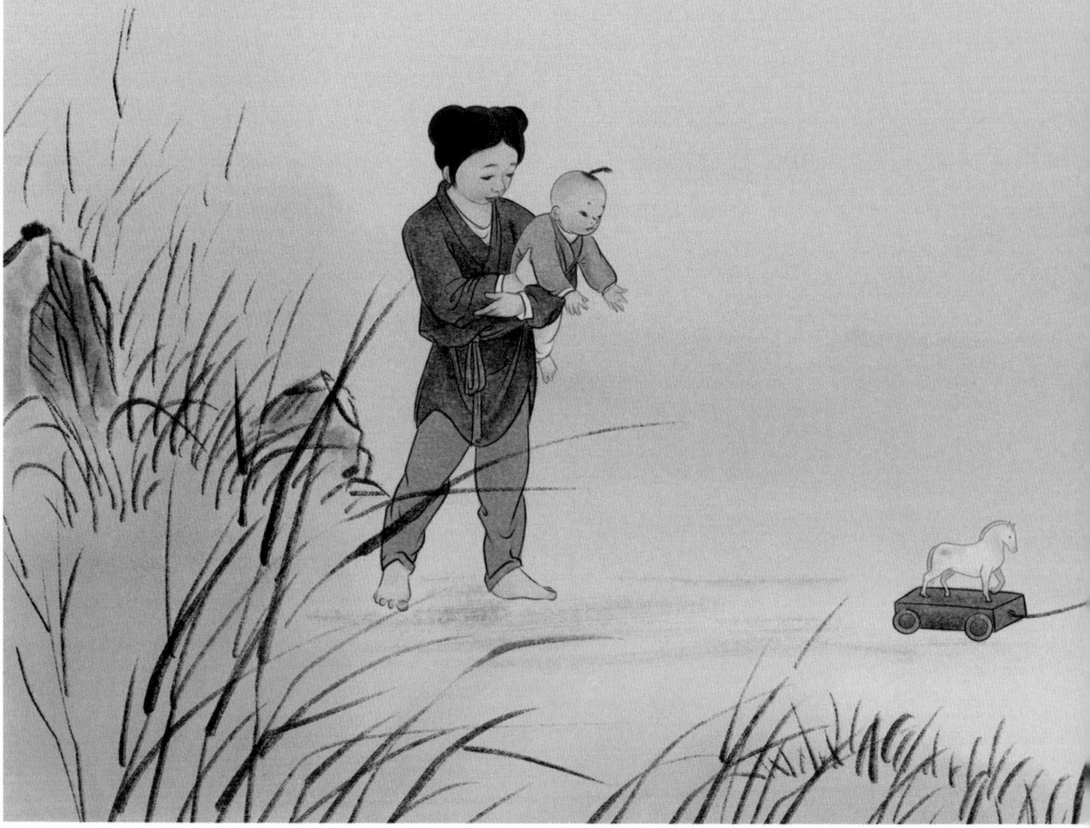

"I don't think you live free
because you have a future.
It's rather because you
don't have a past."

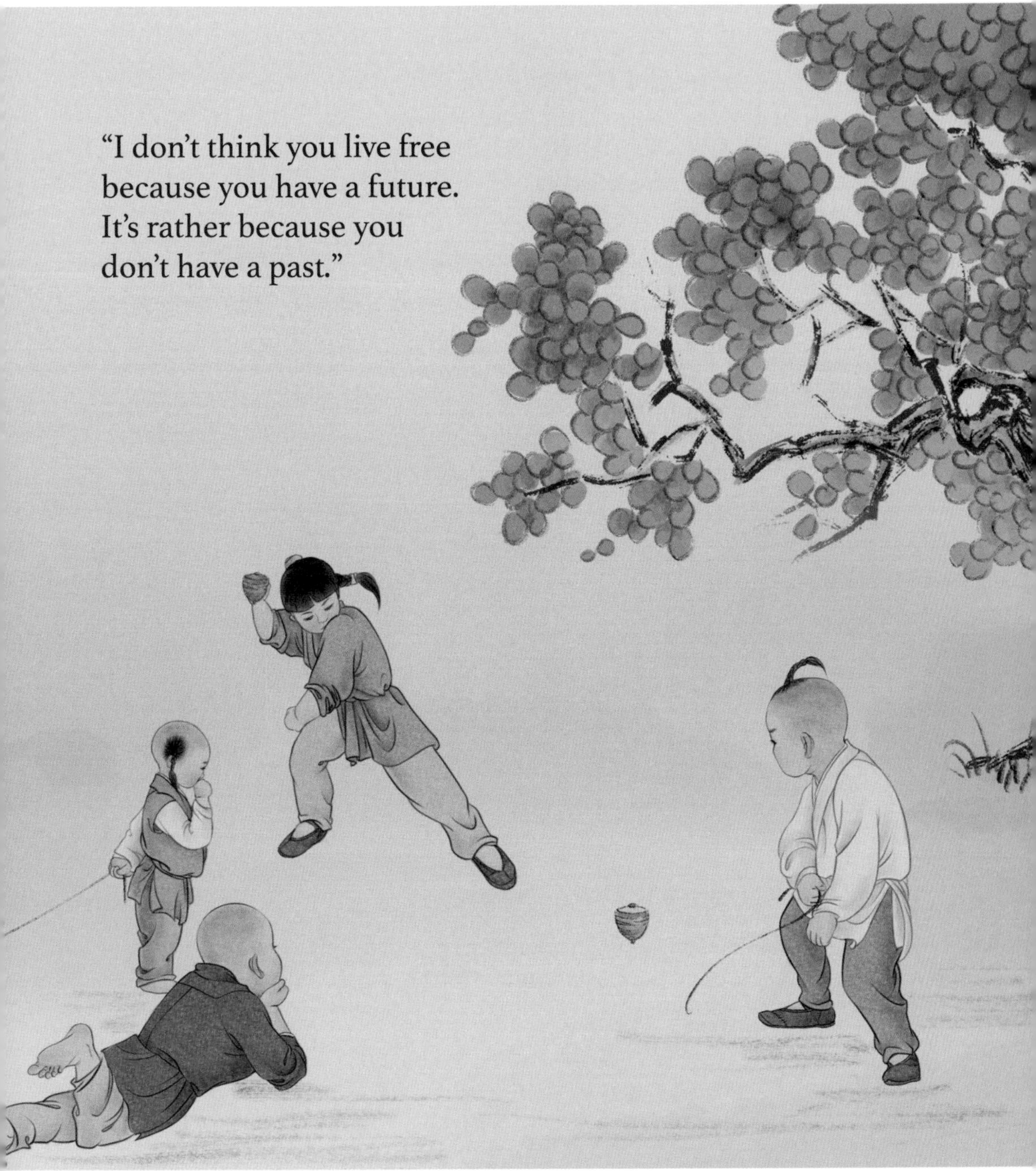

The boy furrowed his brow.
"But I will . . . someday."

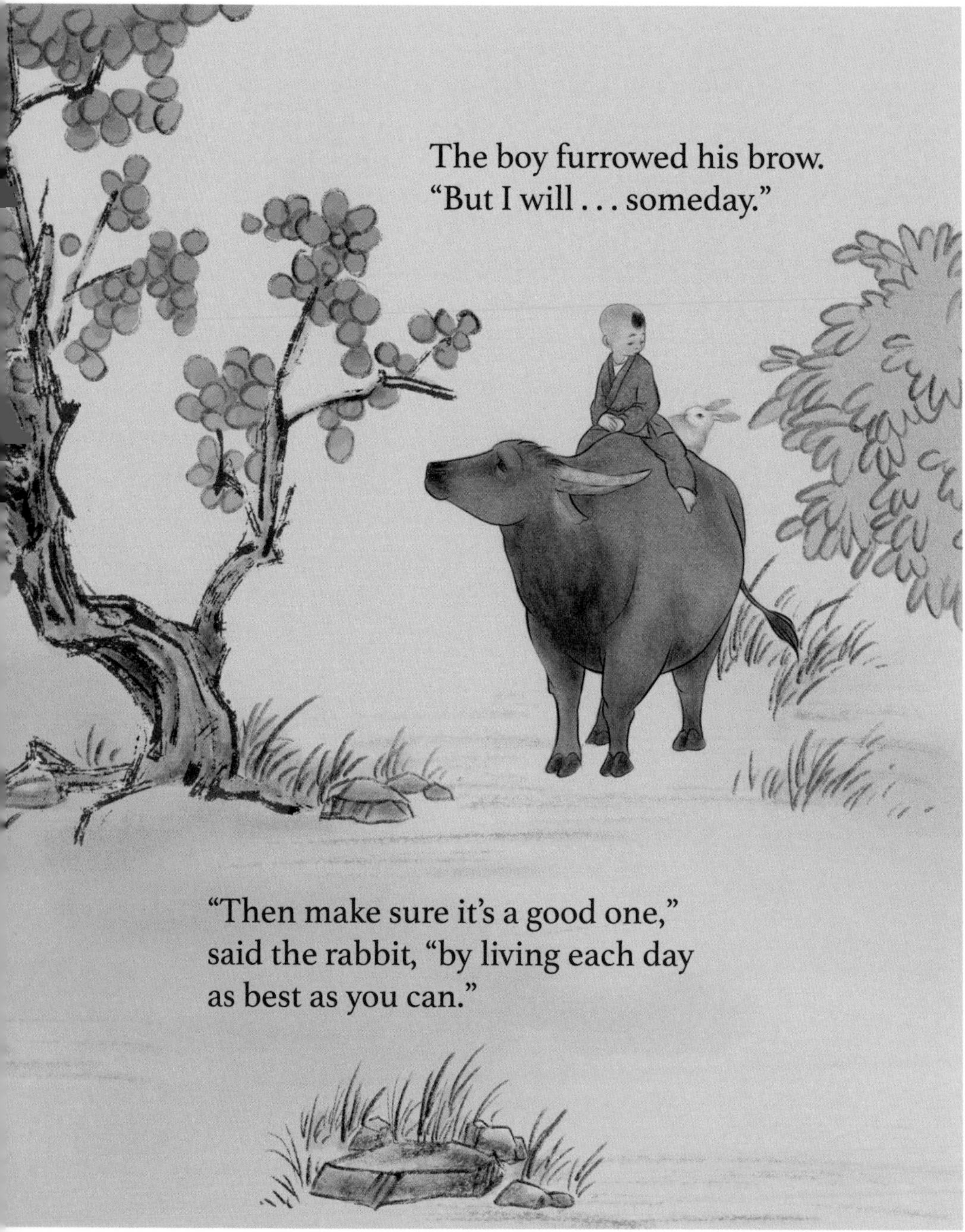

"Then make sure it's a good one,"
said the rabbit, "by living each day
as best as you can."

"He said he's off to find himself, but what does that mean?"

The rabbit tilted her head. "I don't know," she replied. "No one can be found. We can only be created, and we create ourselves every day."

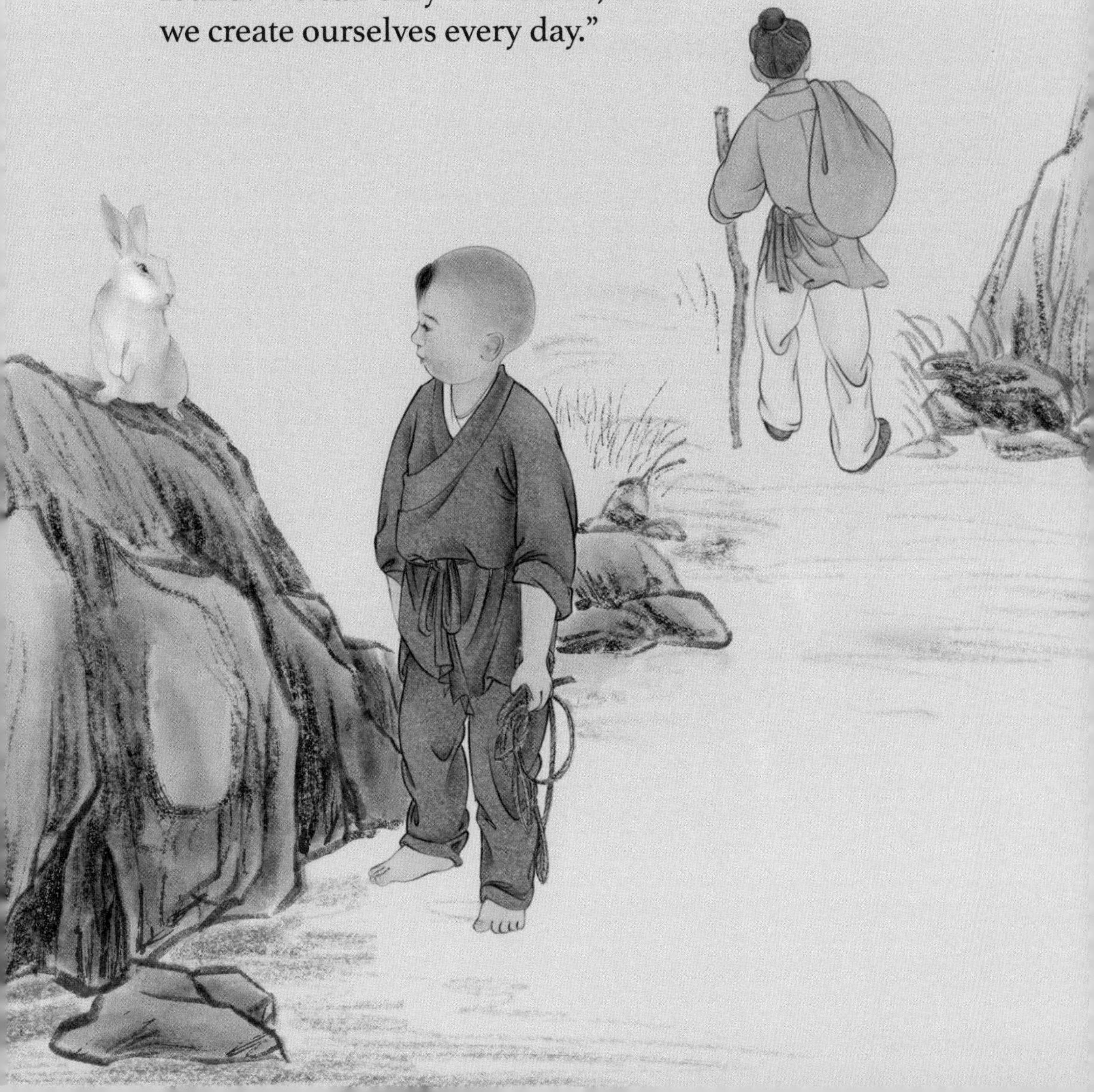

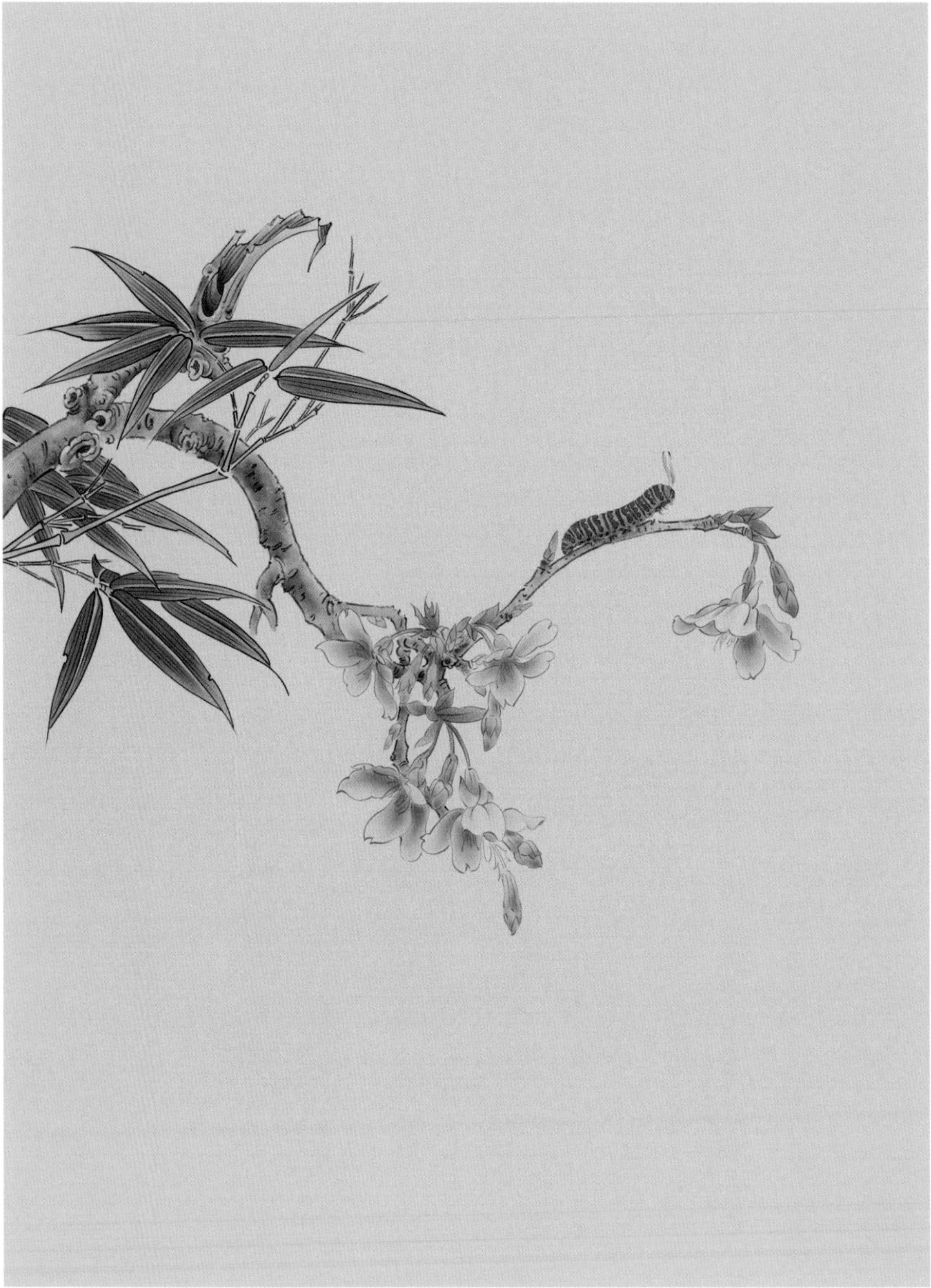

Holding fast to what we are,
keeps us from transforming into
what we might become.

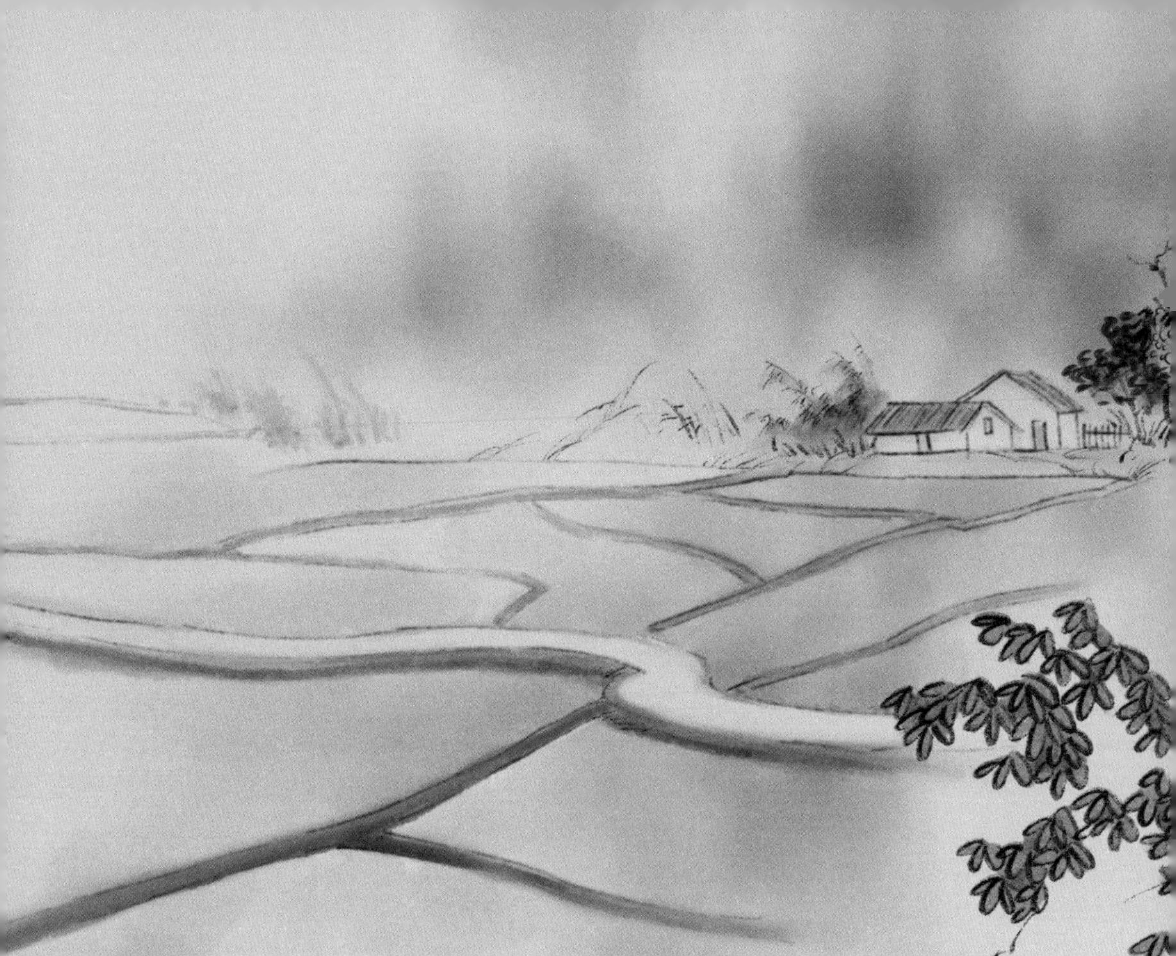

The friends didn't always agree, so they learned from each other instead.

"Paying attention to what's *around* us helps us understand what we really are," said the ox as he lumbered across the bridge.

"And what's that?" asked the boy.

"Inseparable," he replied.

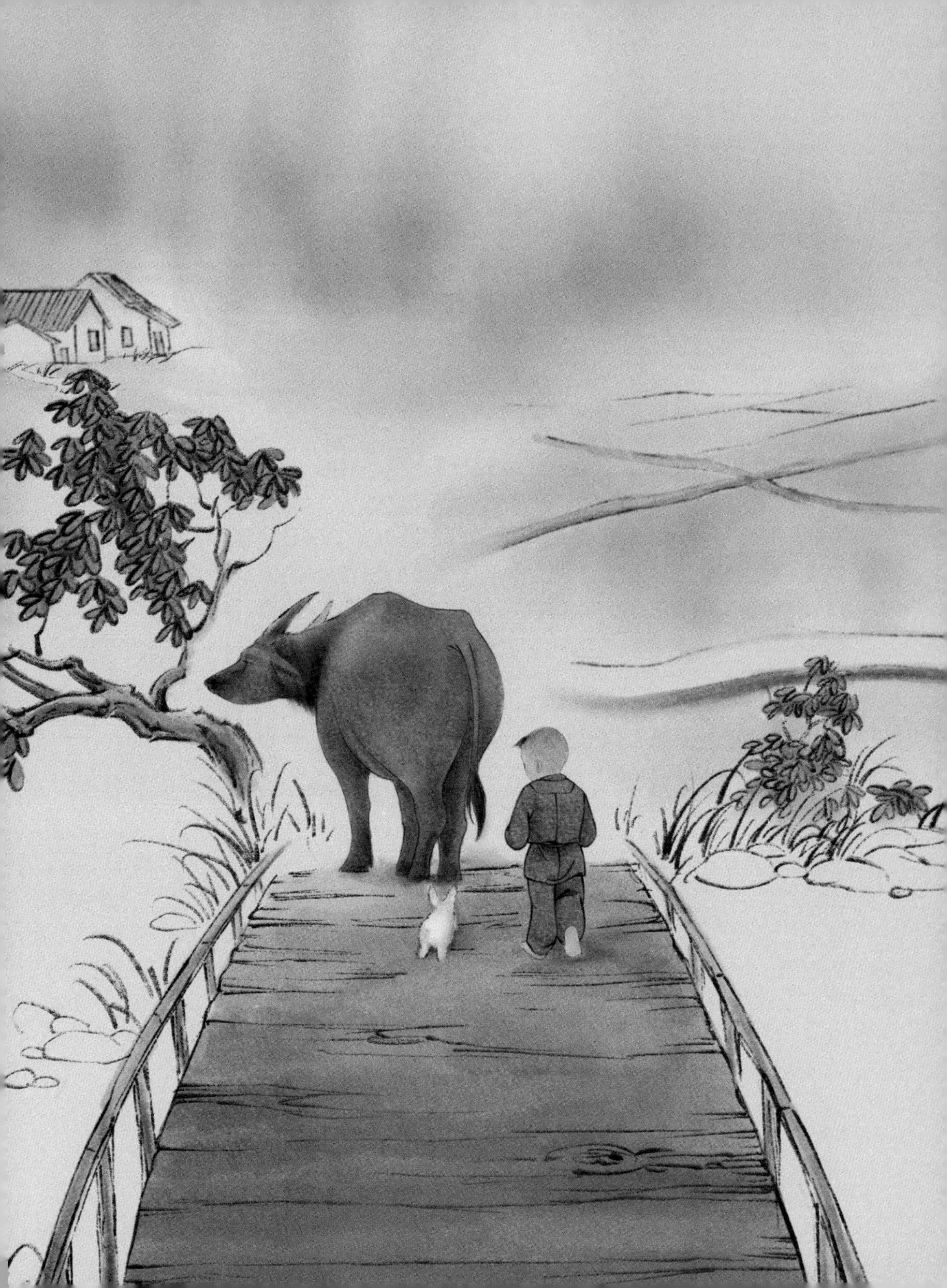

“I think,” said the rabbit, “that if we wonder often, the gift of knowledge will come.”

The oxherd boy gazed at the valley below. “I just hope we don’t lose the gift of wonder.”

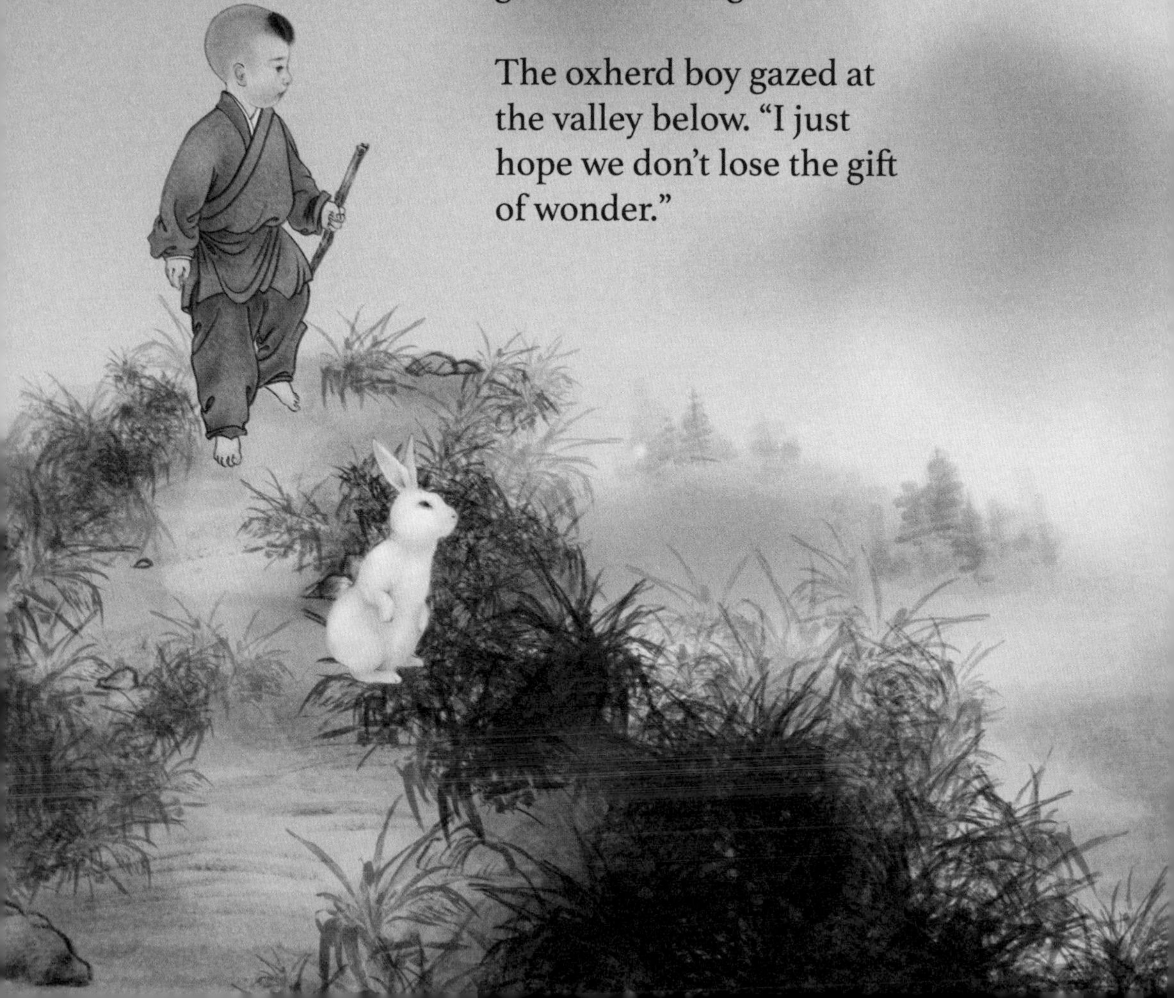

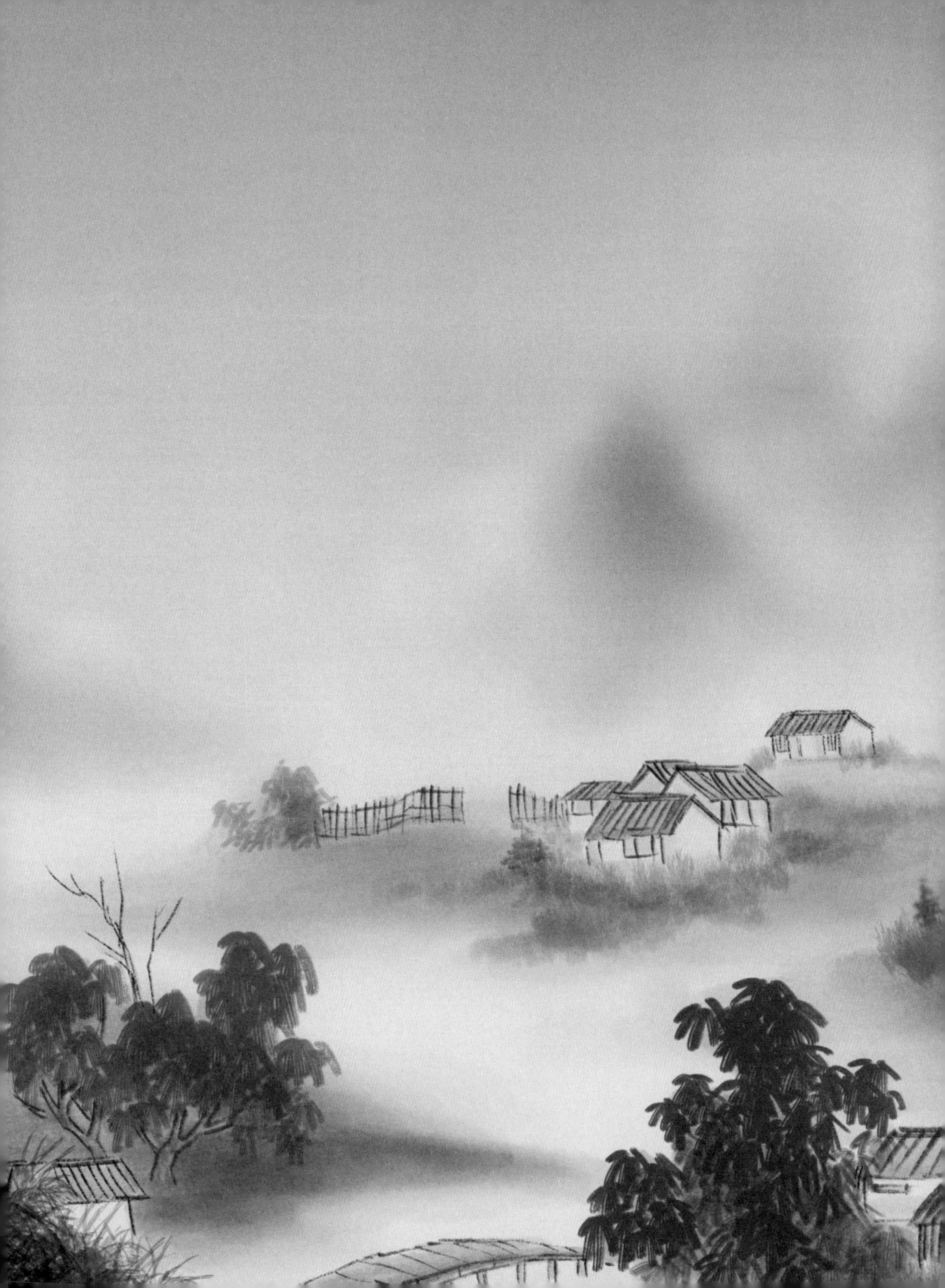

"I thought we were going to enjoy our picnic when we arrived at the top."

"Oh." The oxherd boy chewed thoughtfully. "I thought it'd be nice to celebrate every step."

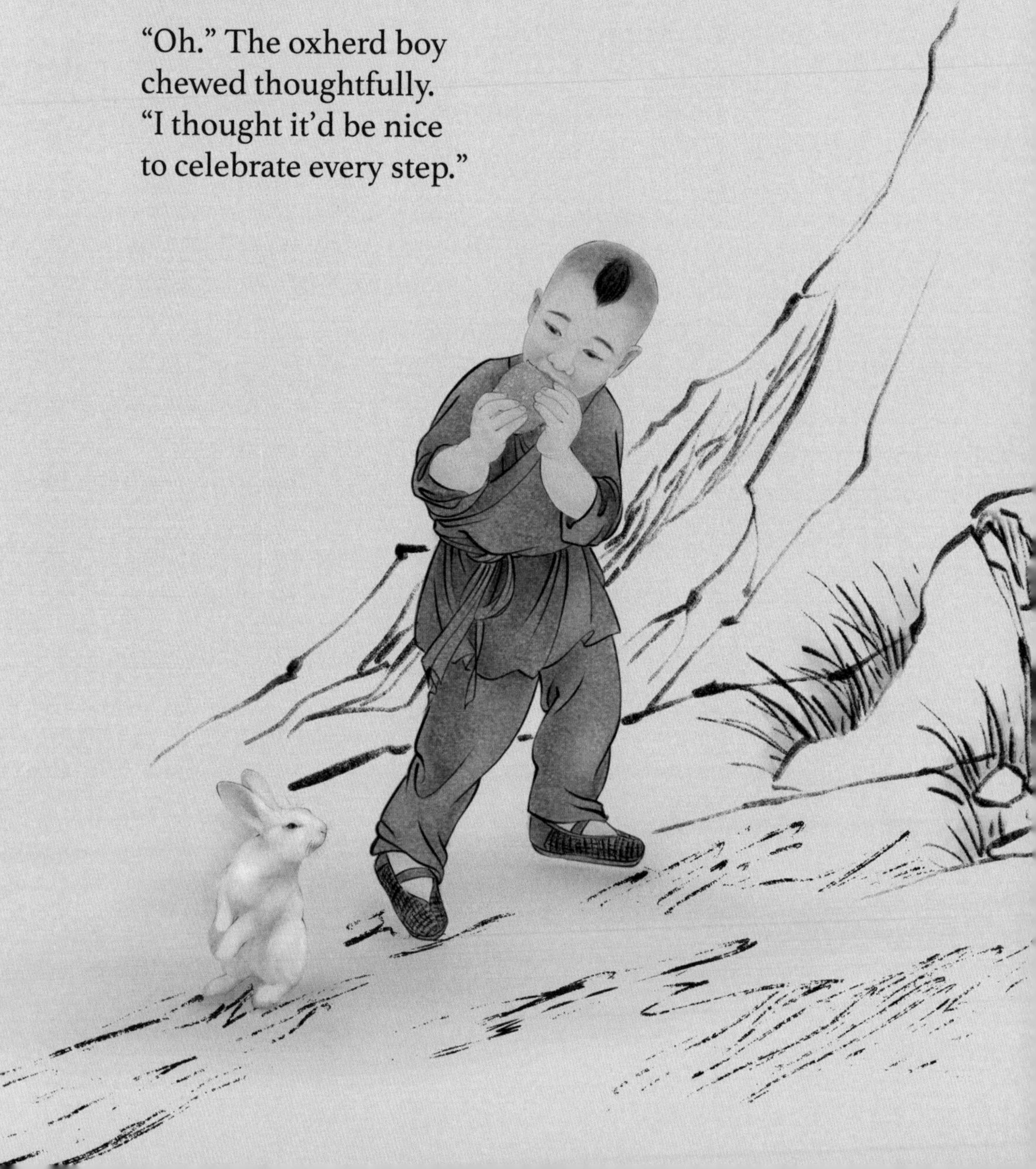

"Everyone just wants to be happy
these days," the rabbit said with a huff.

"Sometimes," responded the ox,
"when we say we want to be happy,
what we really want is to be healed."

The rabbit studied the oxherd boy before asking him, "You could be friends with anyone, so why do you choose to be friends with us?"

"I don't know," he replied. "Maybe it's because when I'm with you, I realize I need very little to be happy."

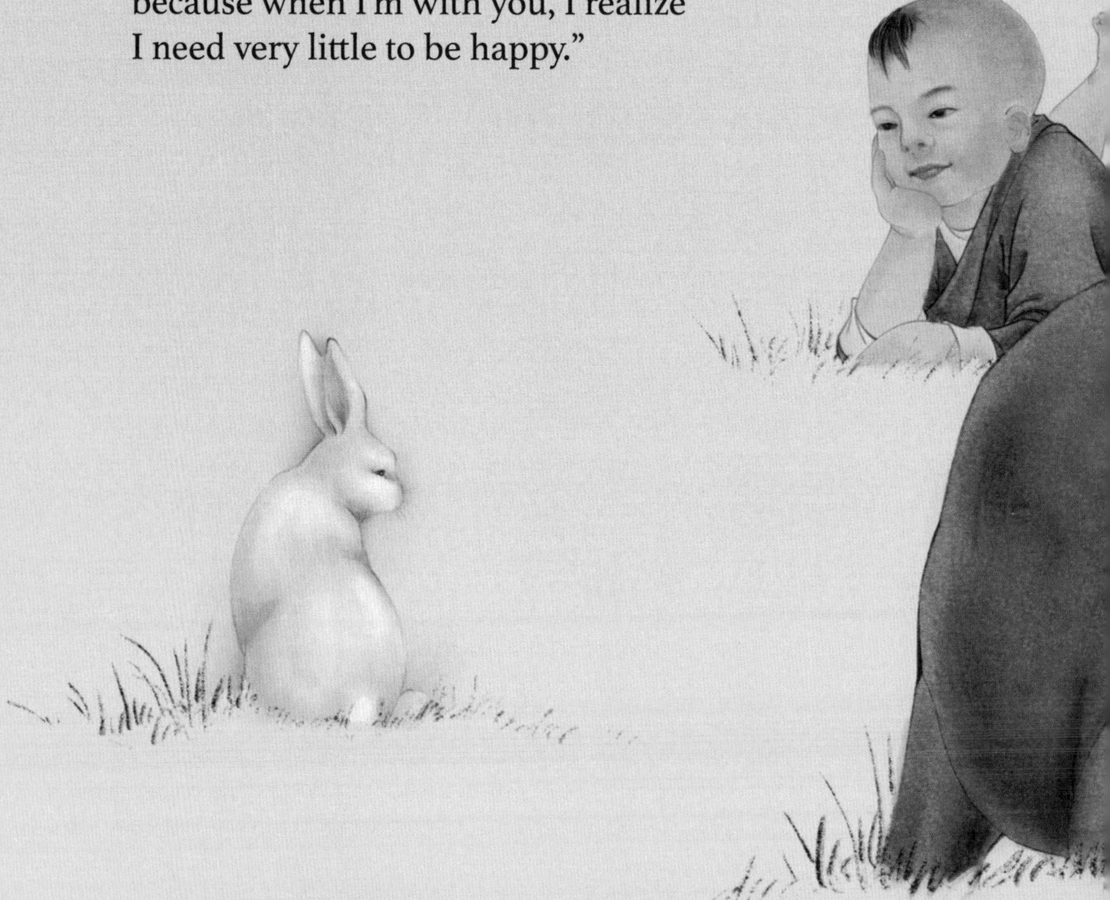

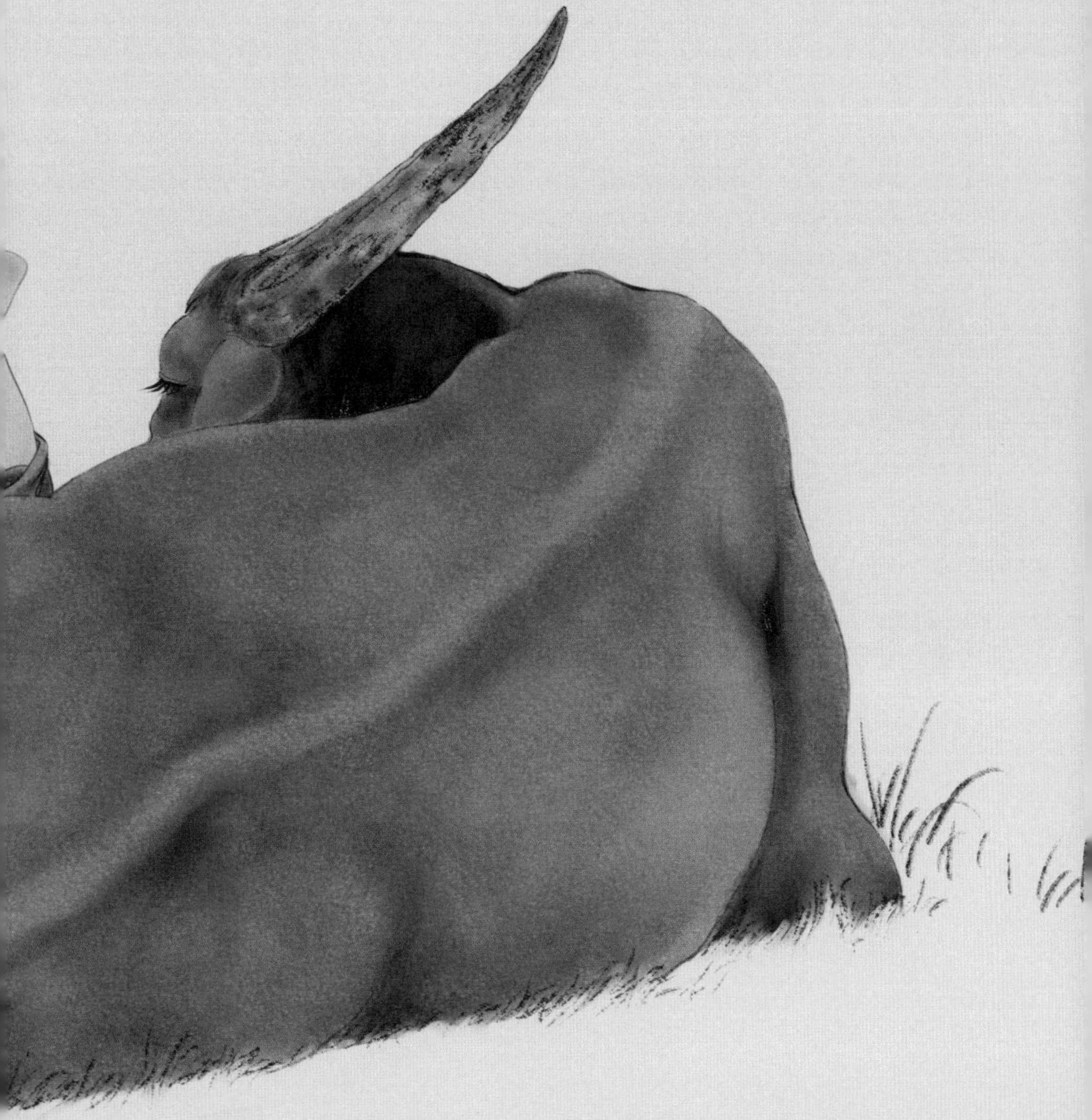

Happiness can be a skill.

Happiness can be
a memory.

Happiness can be
everywhere.

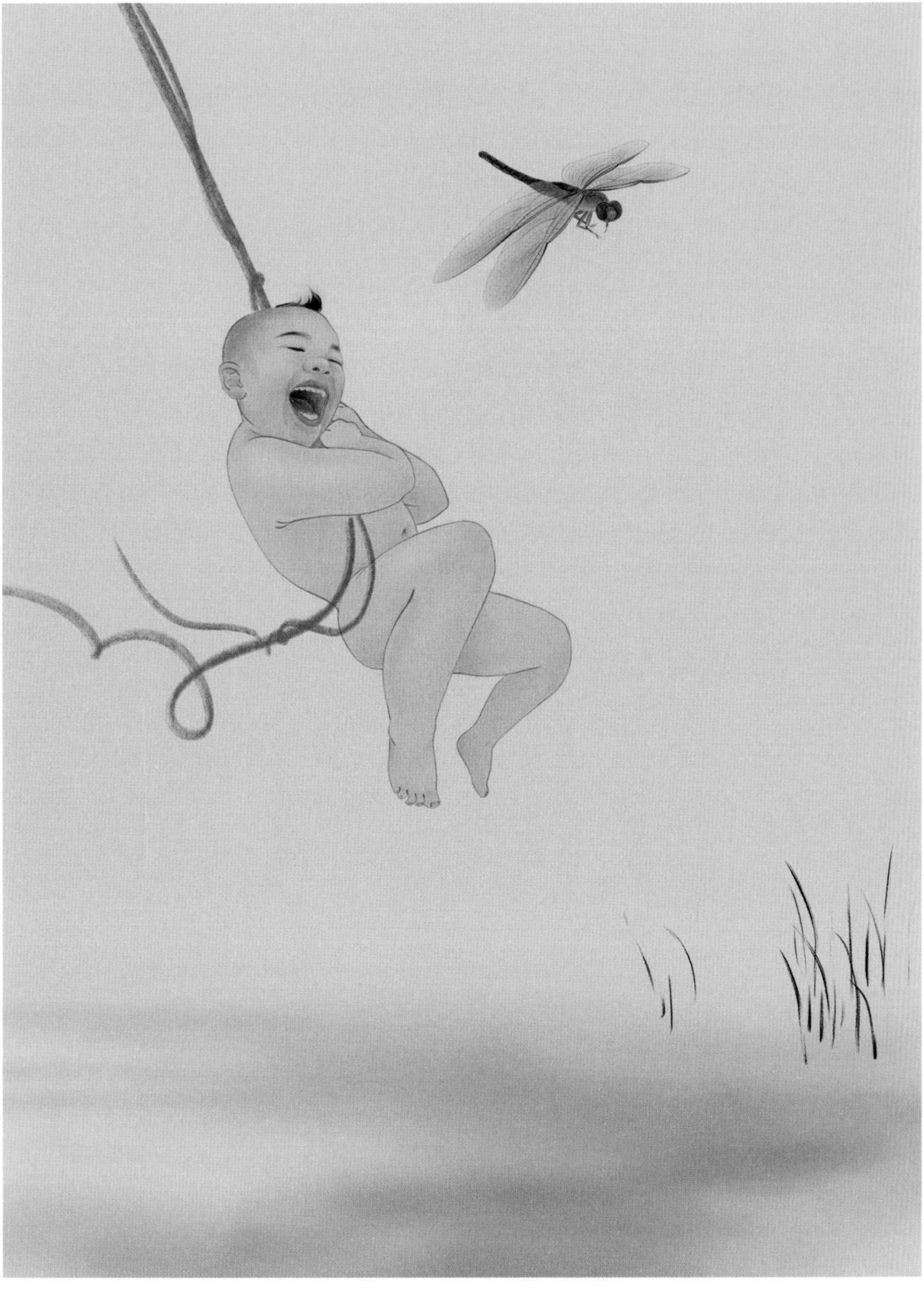

Some moments felt very short for the rabbit, as she sighed softly. "I wish this could last forever."

"Things don't have to last forever to be meaningful."

The rabbit sighed again. "I suppose most things are meaningful because they don't."

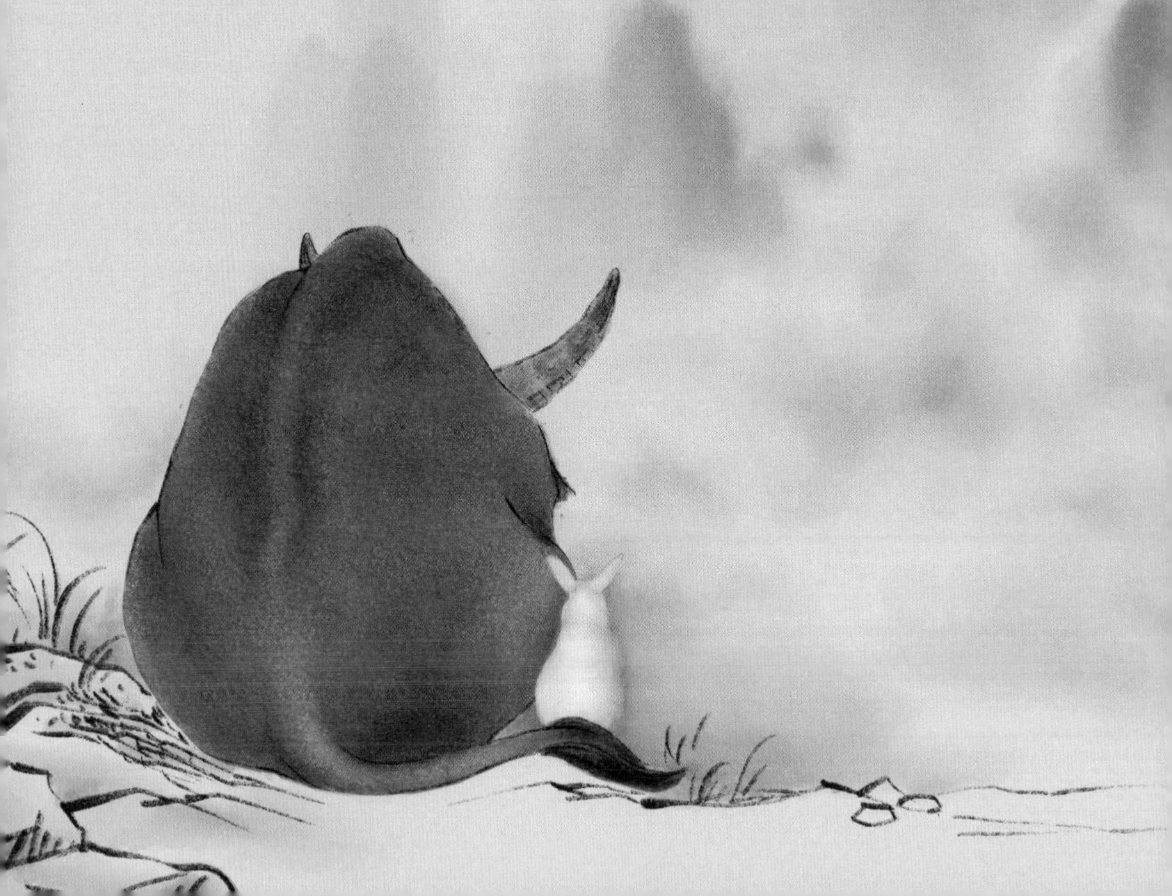

"Ox?"

"Yes, rabbit?" He drew closer until their noses touched.

"I'm so glad you're here."

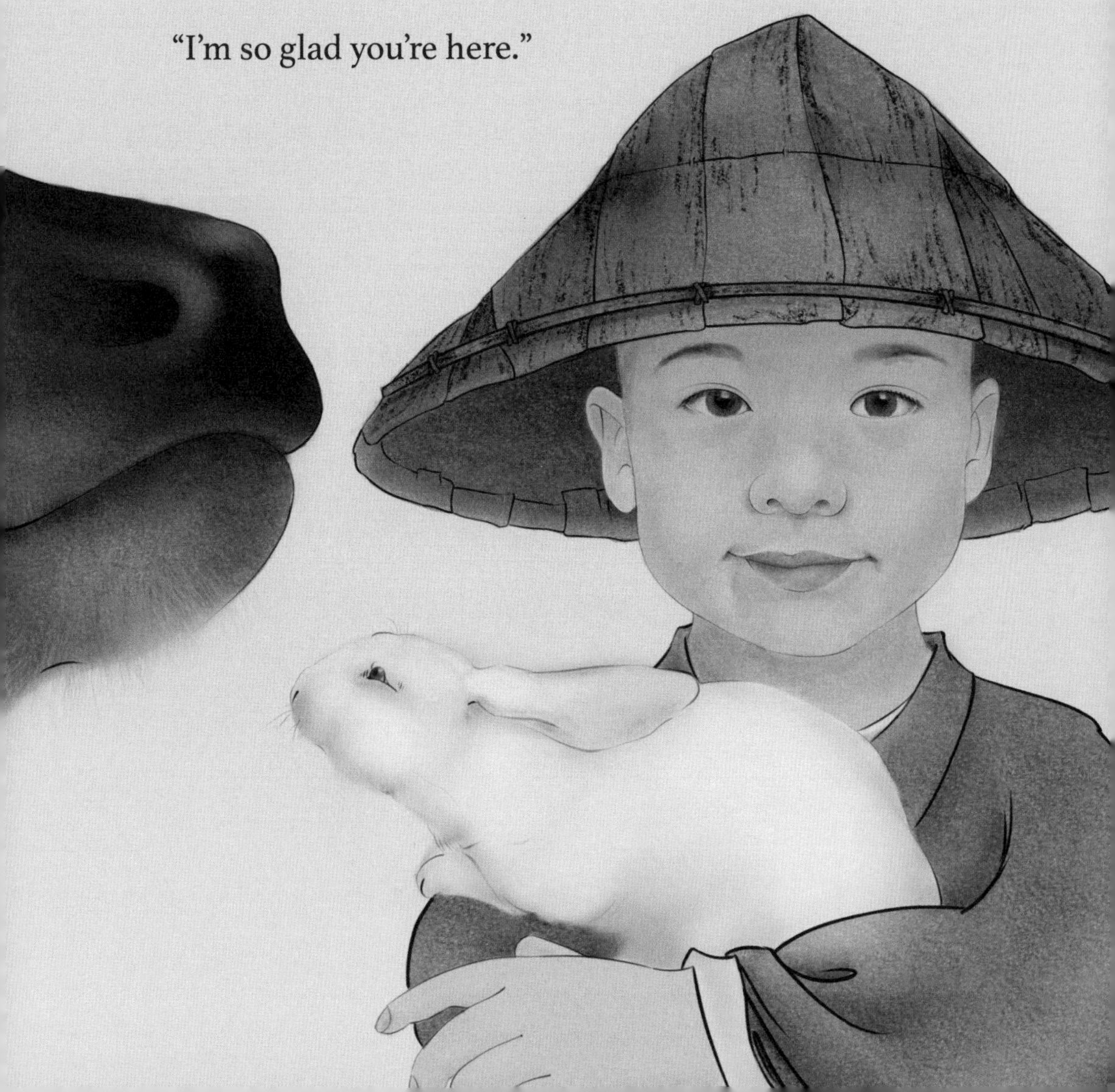

"Sometimes half the battle is finding good friends to run with you in life," observed the boy.

"Oh no, finding good friends to run with you in life is the *entire* battle."

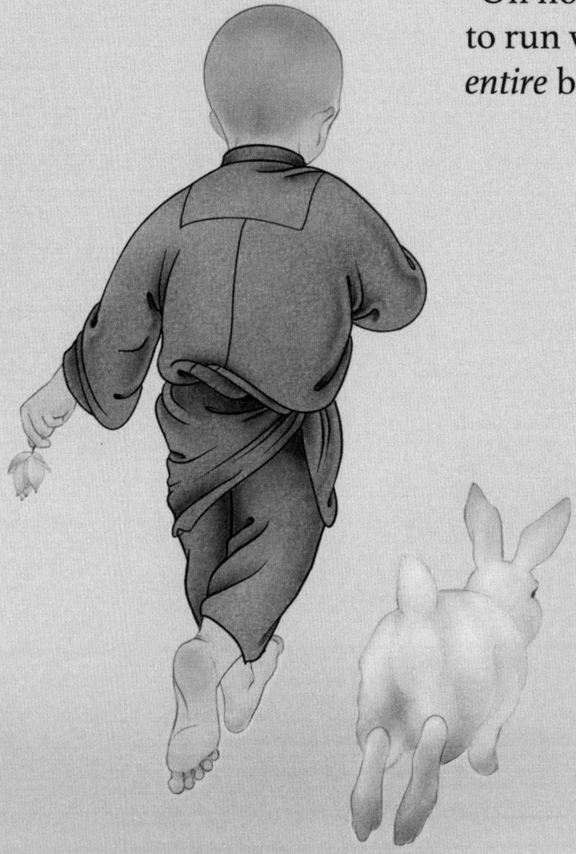

“Are we on the right path?” asked the rabbit.

The oxherd boy looked around. “Maybe there is no path. Maybe the path is made just by walking.”

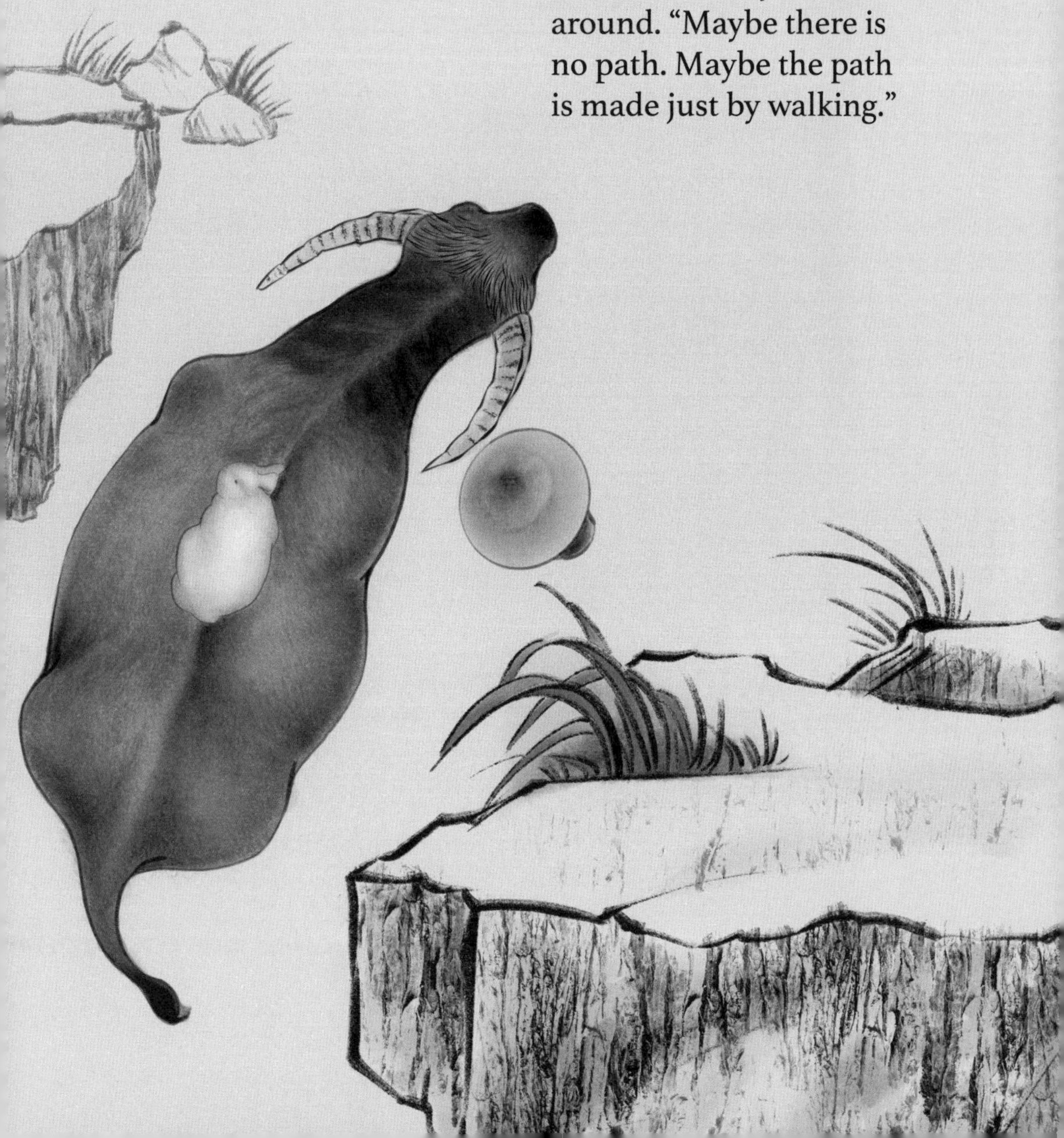

"Thank you for always carrying us," said the oxherd boy.

"Thank *you*," the ox replied, "for carrying me in your own way."

“We’re not making much progress,” the ox said as he struggled against the river.

“Don’t be afraid of going slowly,” comforted the rabbit. “Only be afraid of standing still.”

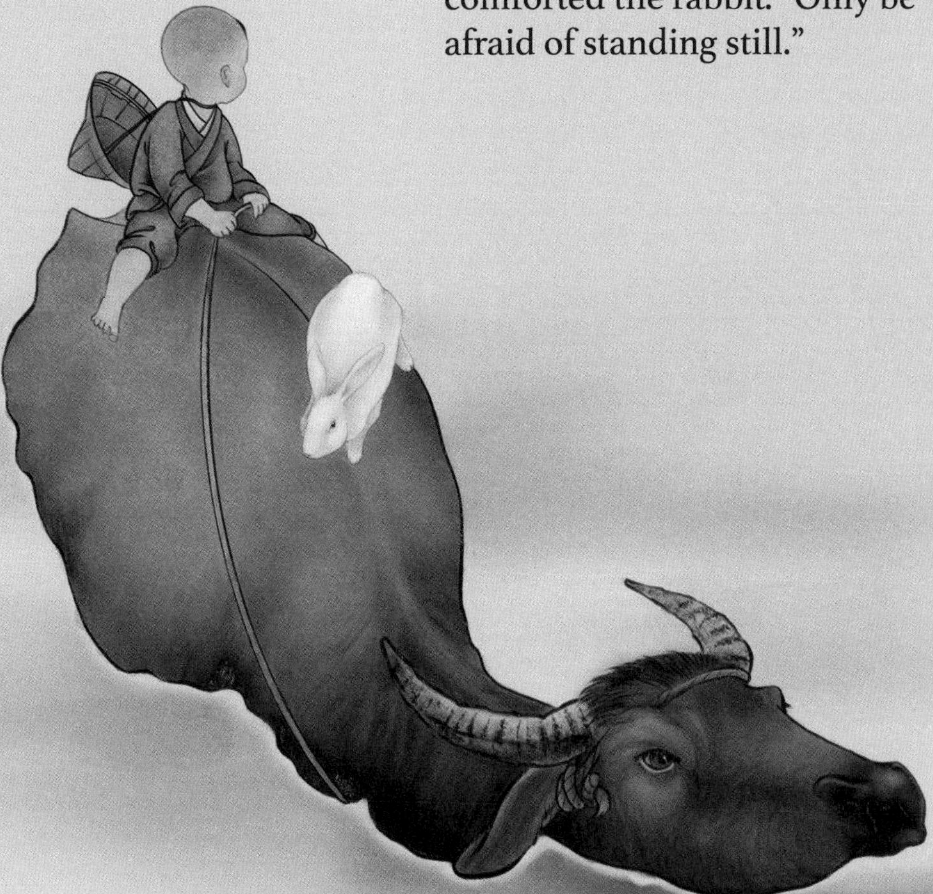

"Do you think the ox is powerful because he's so strong?" the rabbit asked the oxherd boy.

"No," he replied. "I think the ox is powerful because he's so calm."

"Sometimes I feel like I don't know what I'm doing," the ox admitted quietly.

The boy nodded. "So do I. Maybe that's just a sign that we're alive."

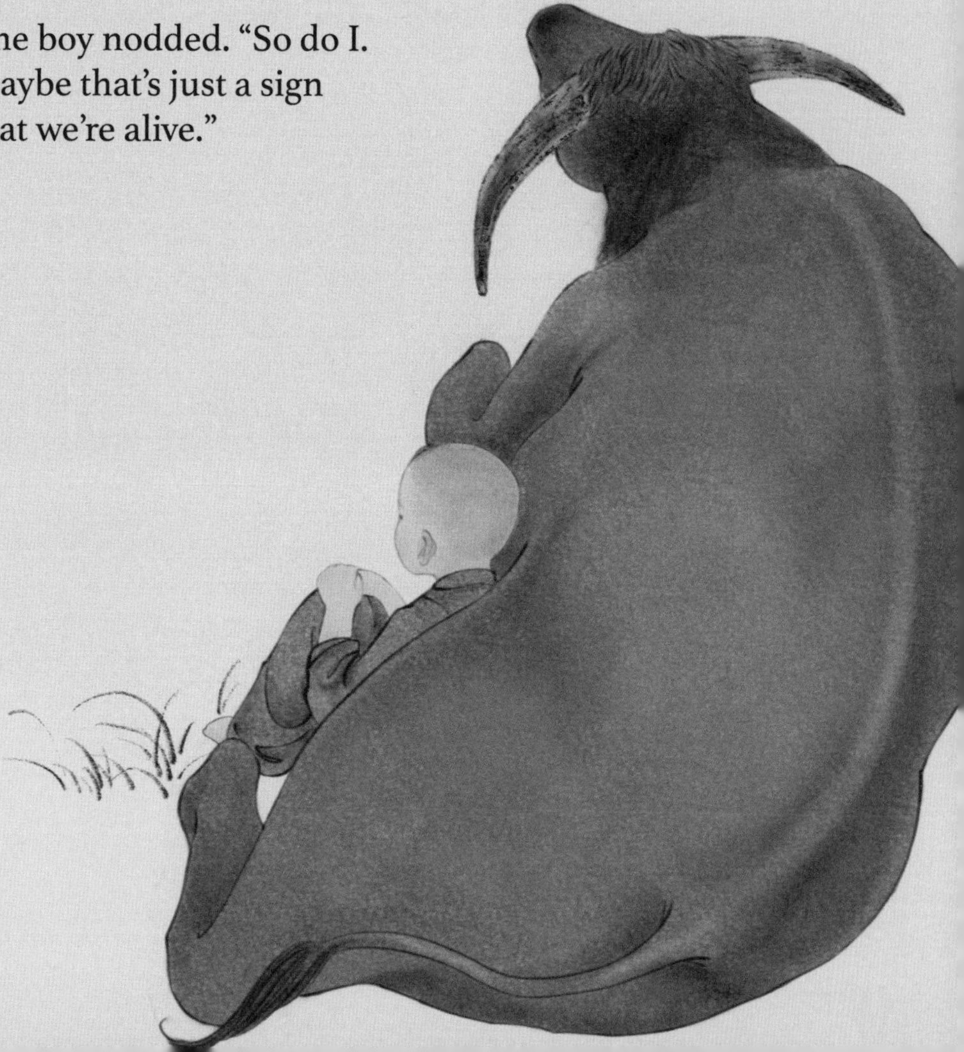

"I will gladly carry you across these deep and troubled waters," said the ox. "But to reach the other shore, you must cling to me no more."

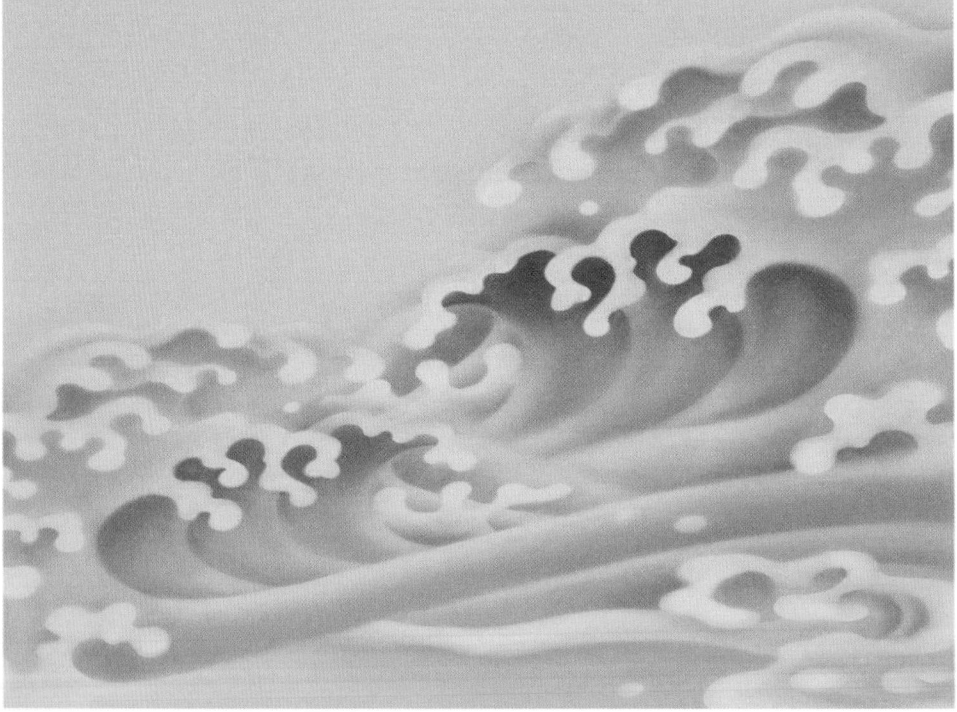

Sometimes you can only do a
small, small thing for yourself.

And that can make all the
difference.

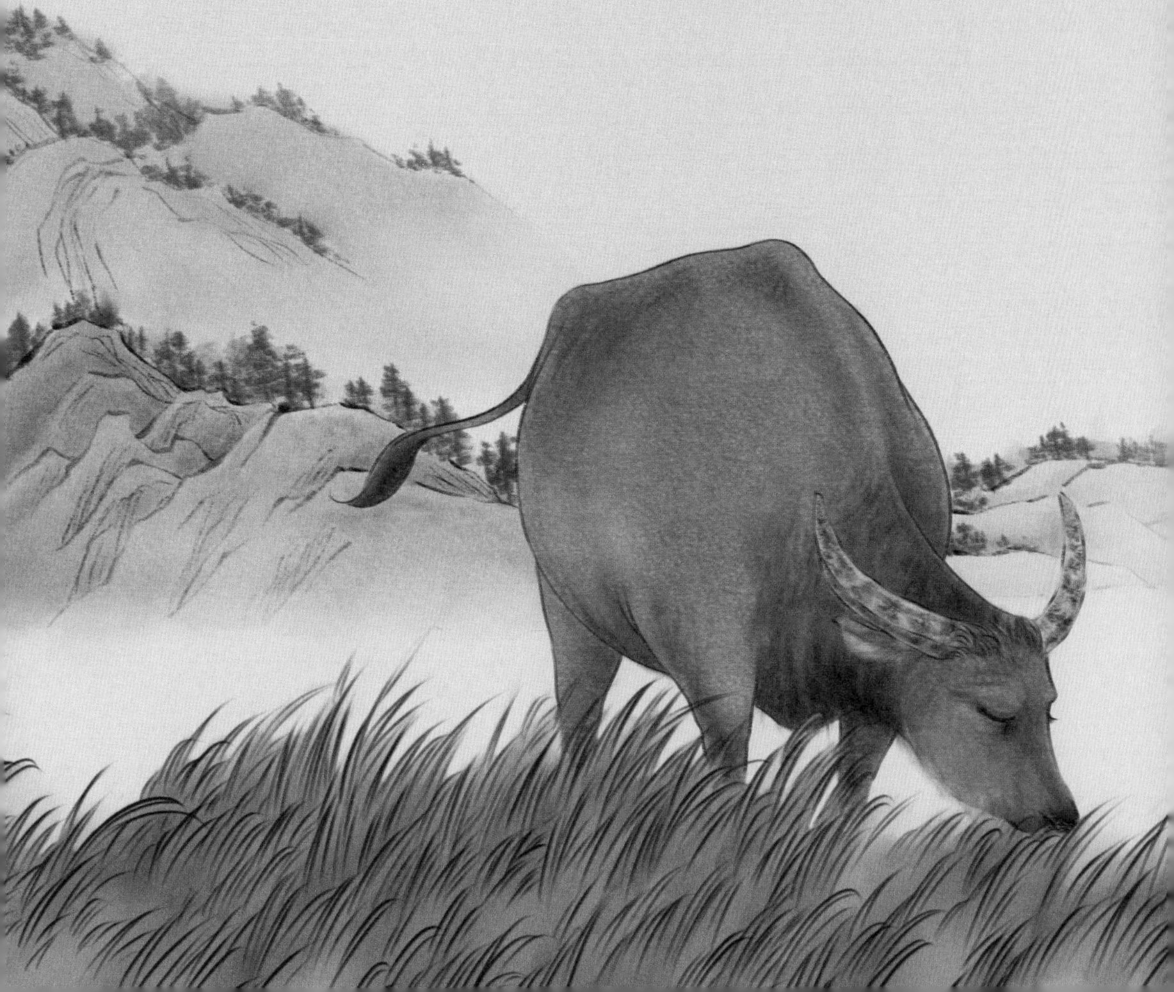

The most difficult choice we can make is whether to be accepted for what we are not, or seen for who we truly are.

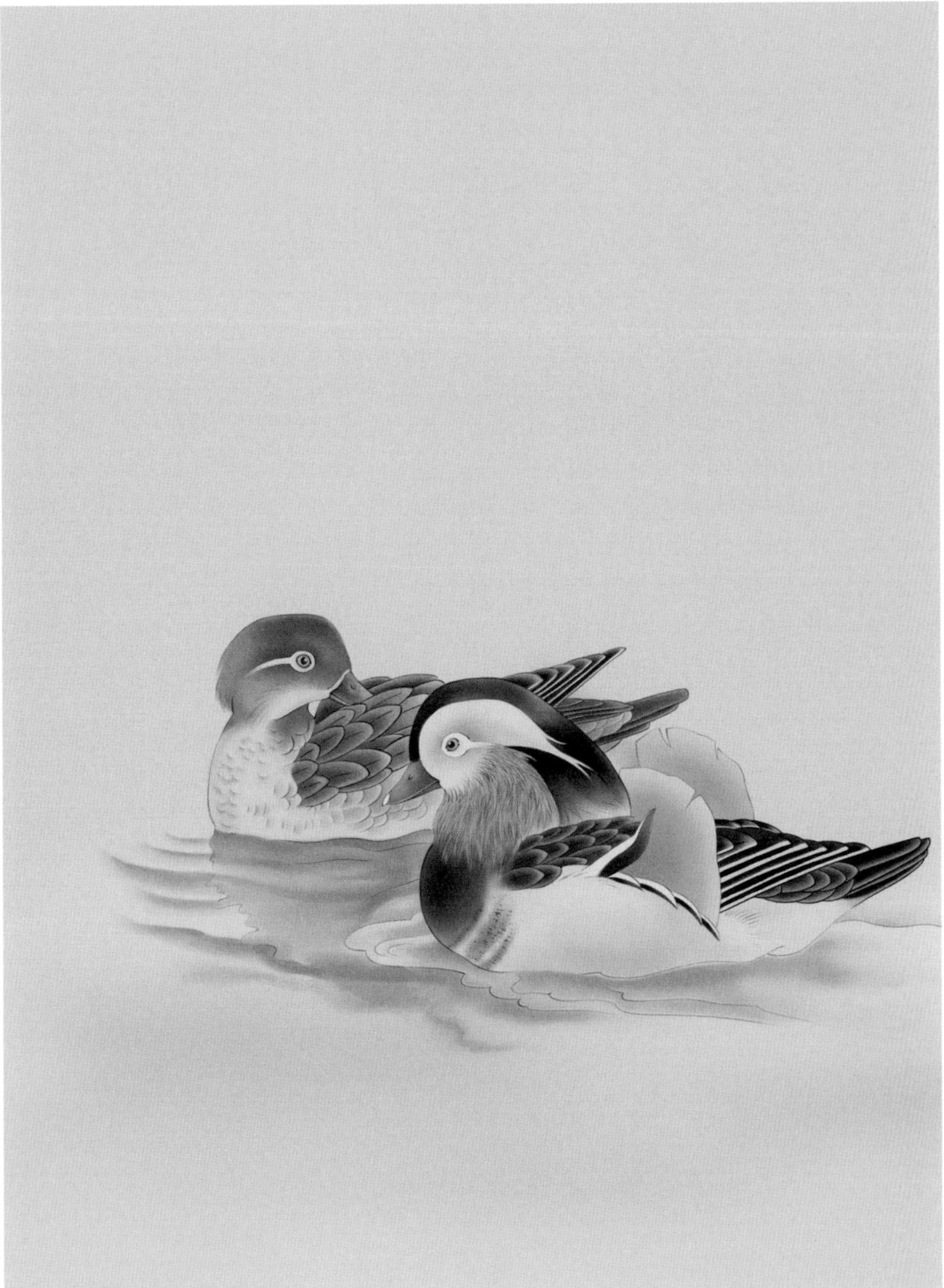

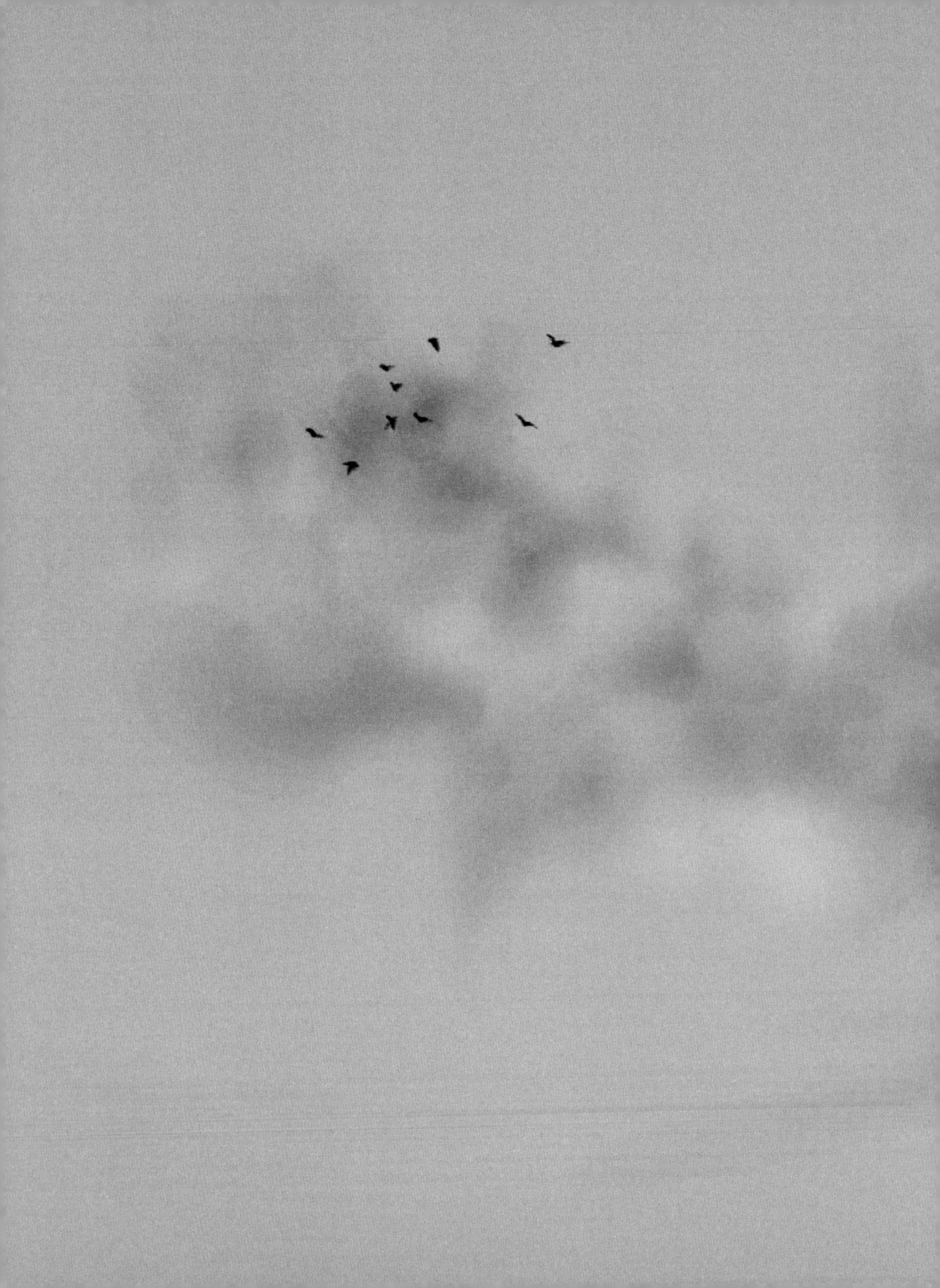

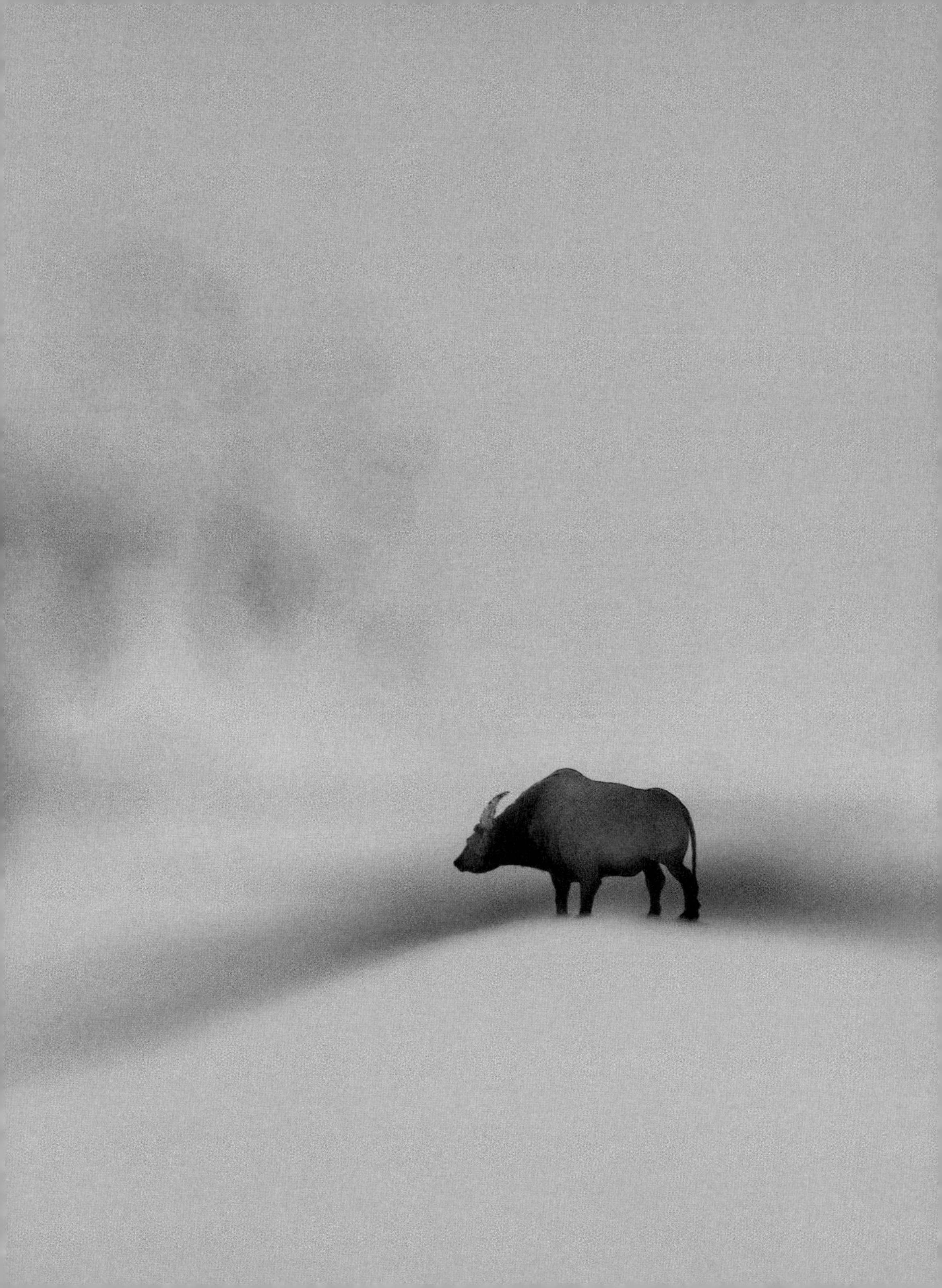

Some moments felt too long for the ox. "I'm in a dark place right now," he said to the rabbit.

"Can I turn on a light for you?"

"No. I'll be all right if someone could stay here with me until it passes."

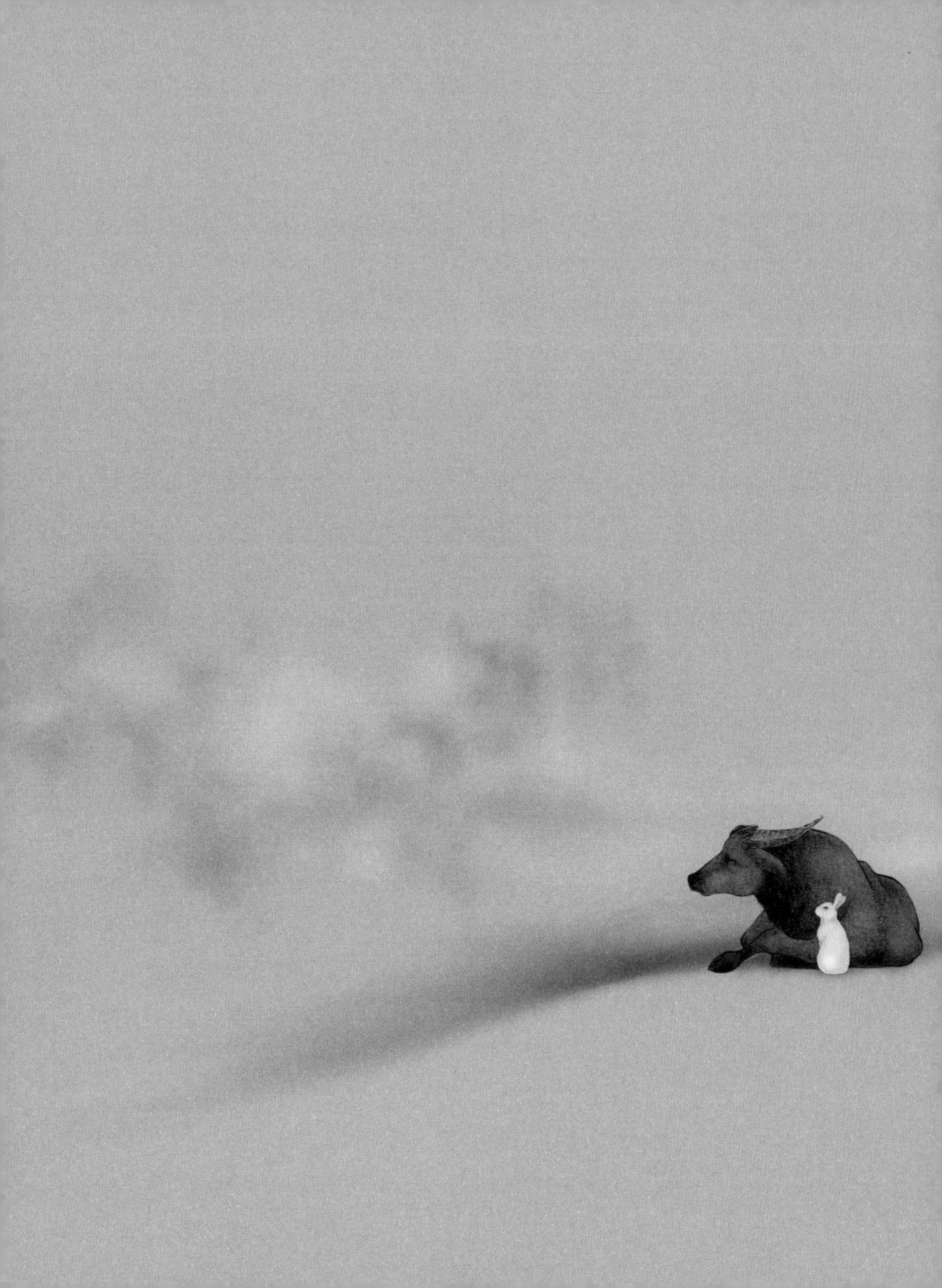

"Thank you," said the ox.

Even so, the ox heaved a sad sigh. "Sometimes my heart is just so heavy with worries."

"Then I will listen until it feels light again."

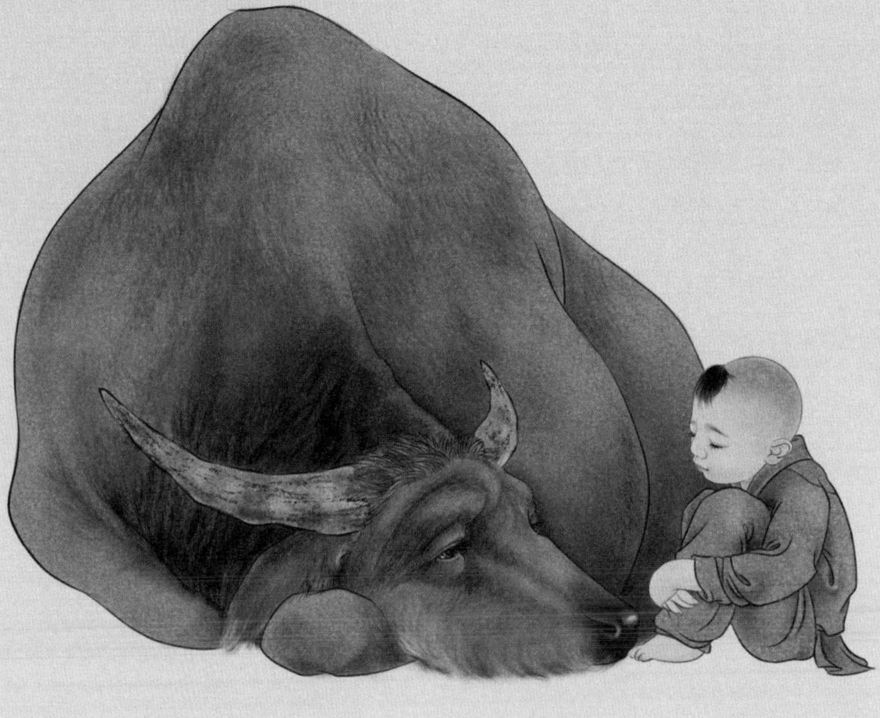

"Sometimes the smallest
words are the ones to save you,"
the rabbit said.

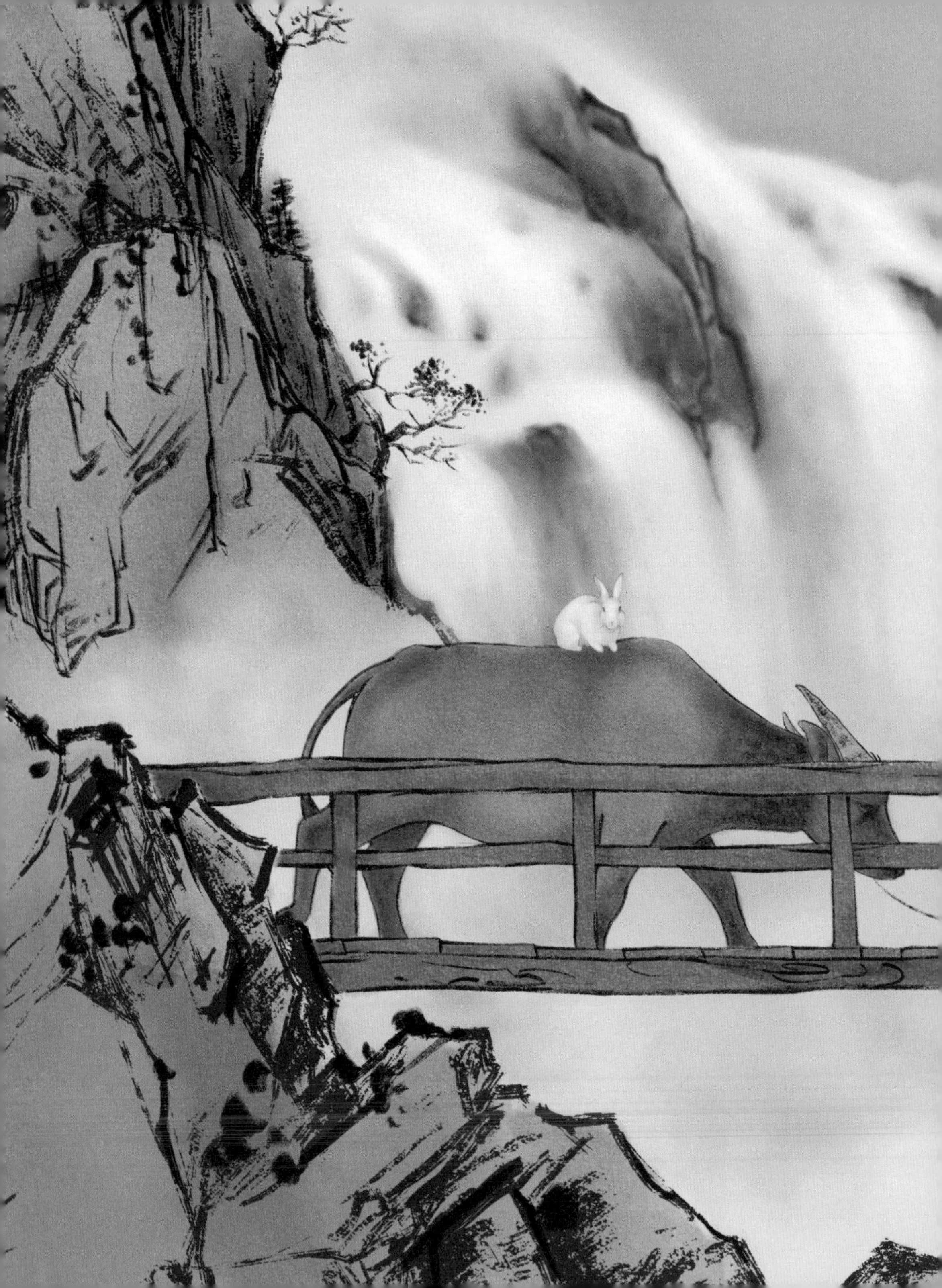

"Do you think time heals all wounds?"
the ox asked the rabbit.

She shook her head and replied,
"I don't think it's time that heals.
It's what we do with time that
makes us better or worse."

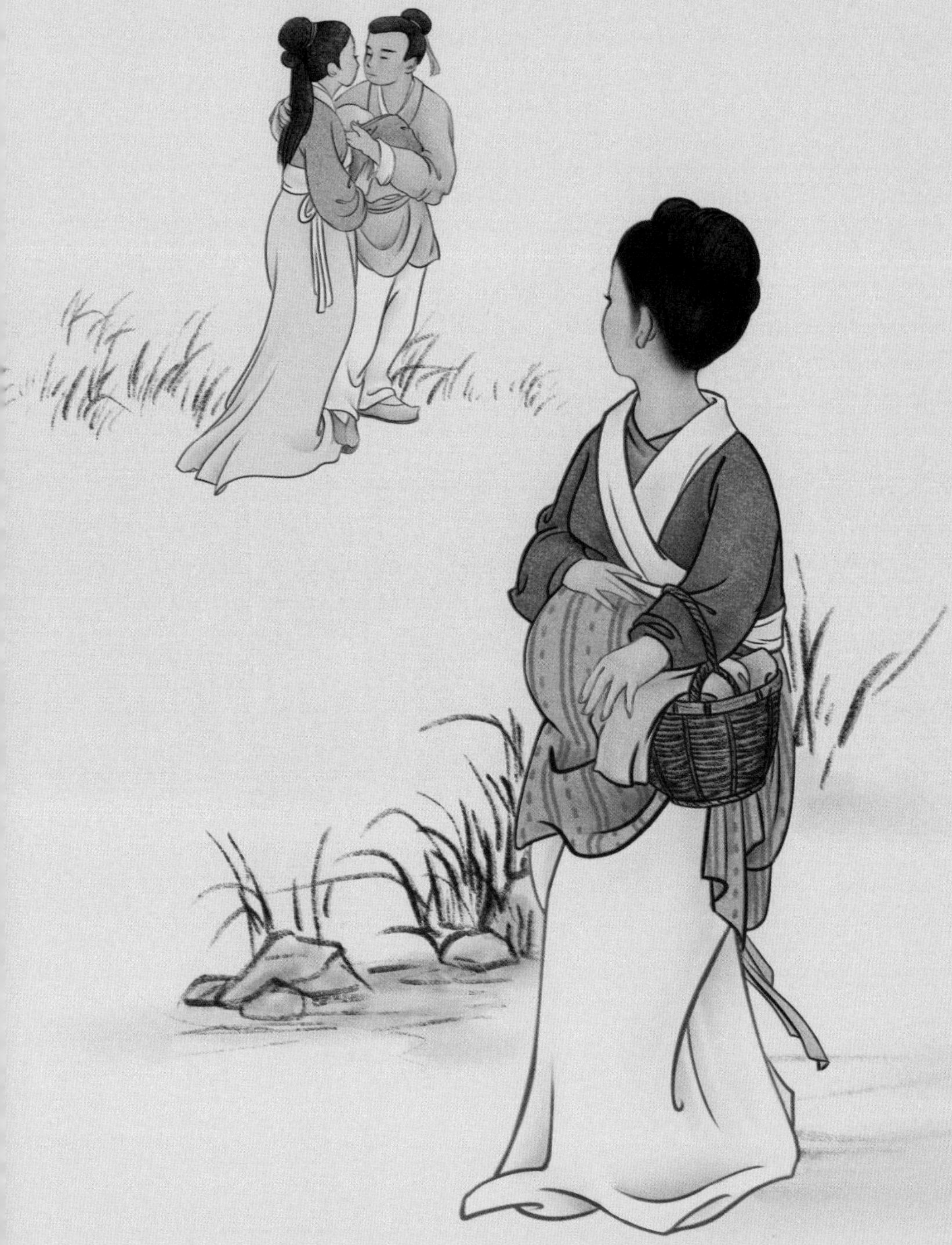

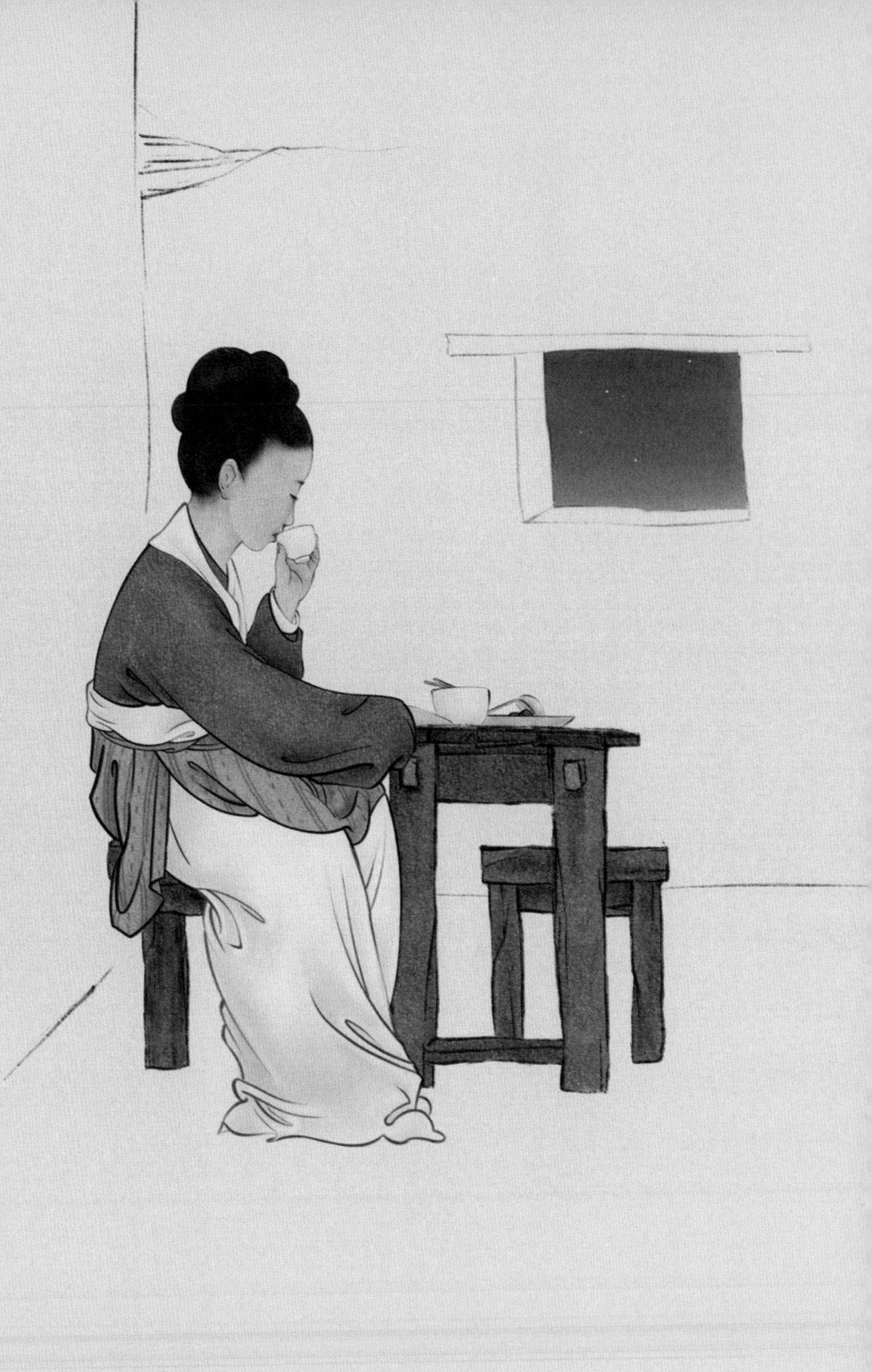

"It makes me sad when others don't get their happily ever after," the rabbit grumbled as they walked home.

The oxherd boy shrugged lightly. "Maybe their happily ever after is the chance to begin again."

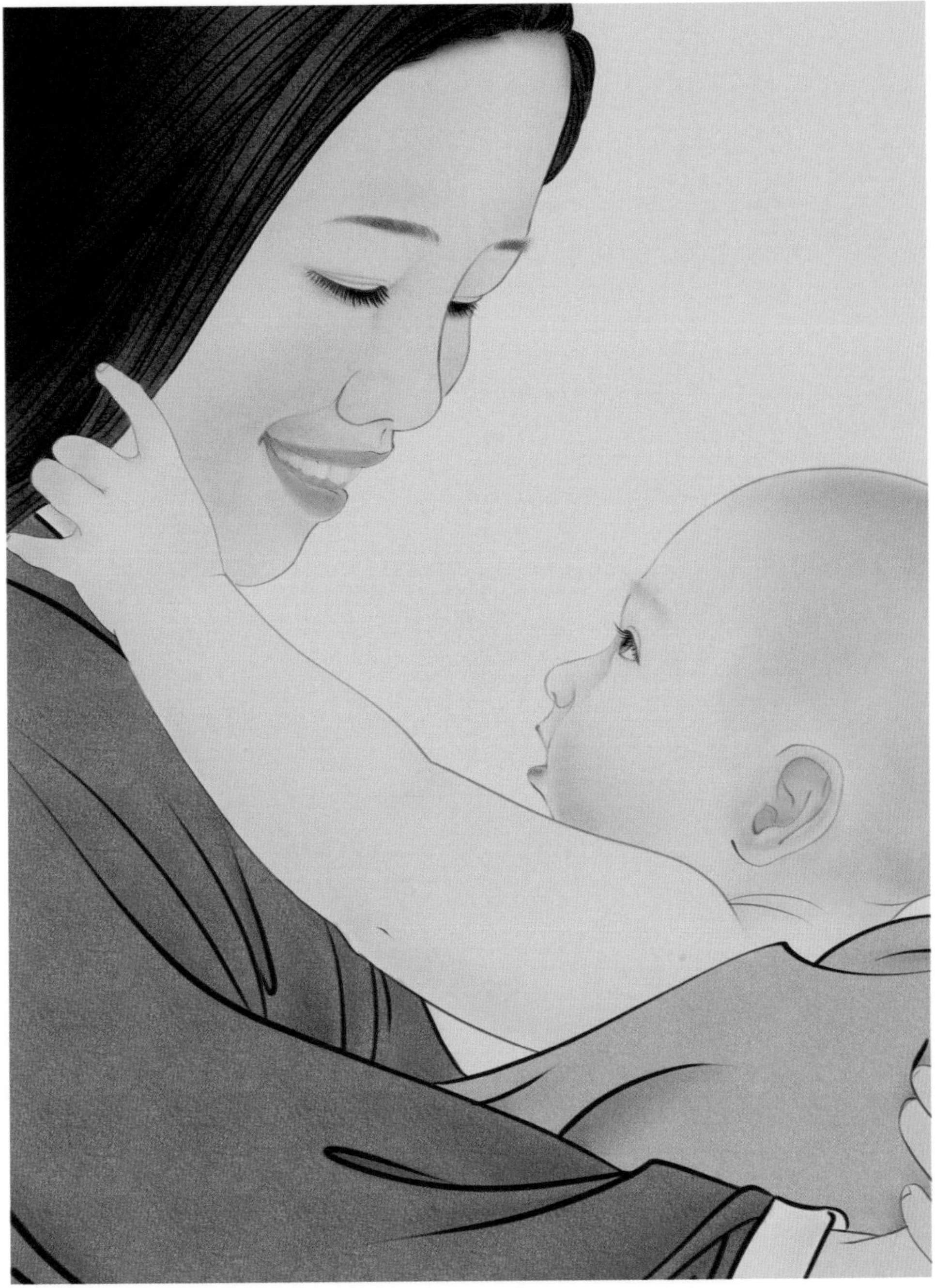

This is the greatest
challenge of being alive:

To witness the injustice
of the world and not allow it
to consume our light.

You are capable of more love
than you can possibly know.

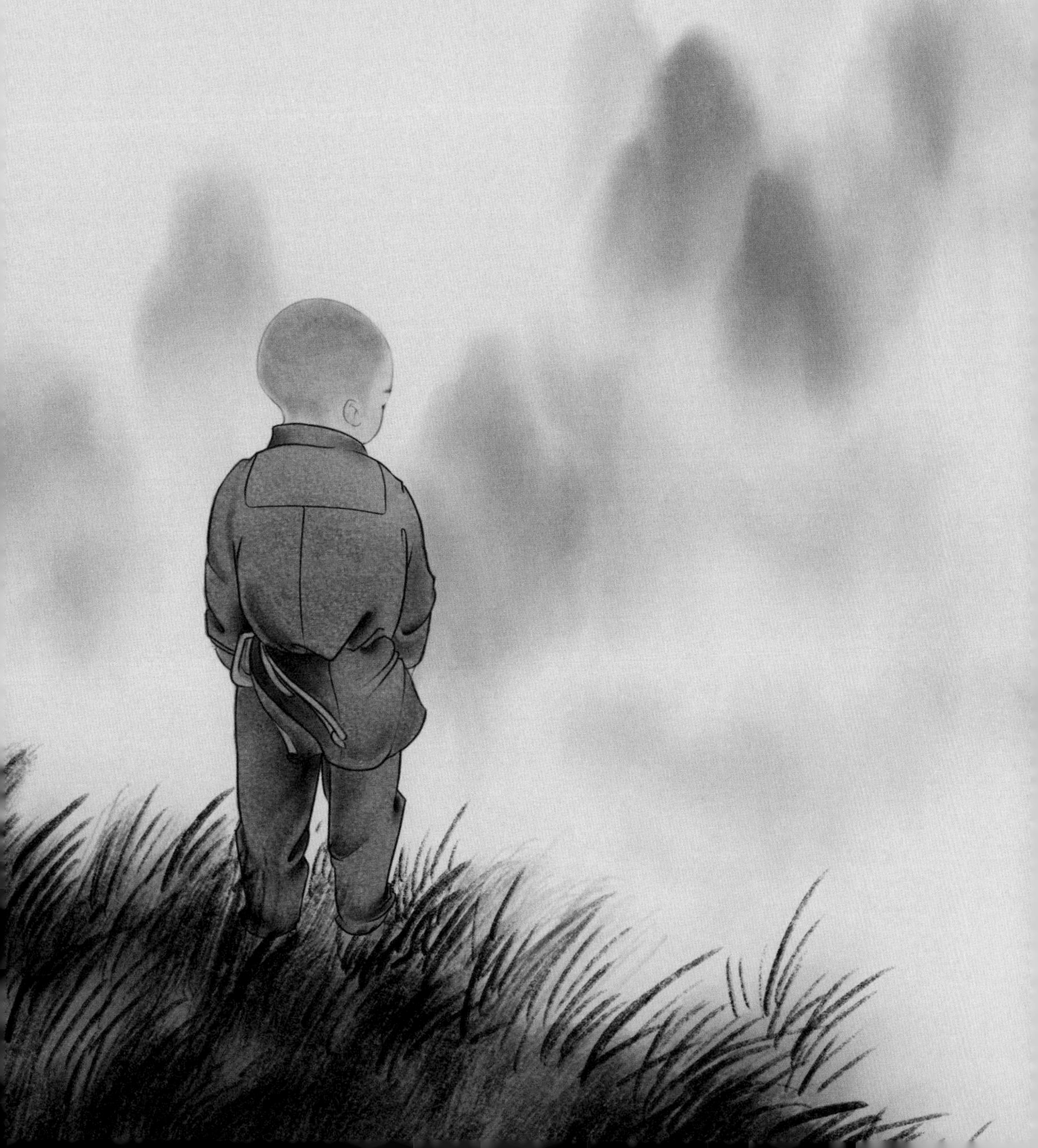

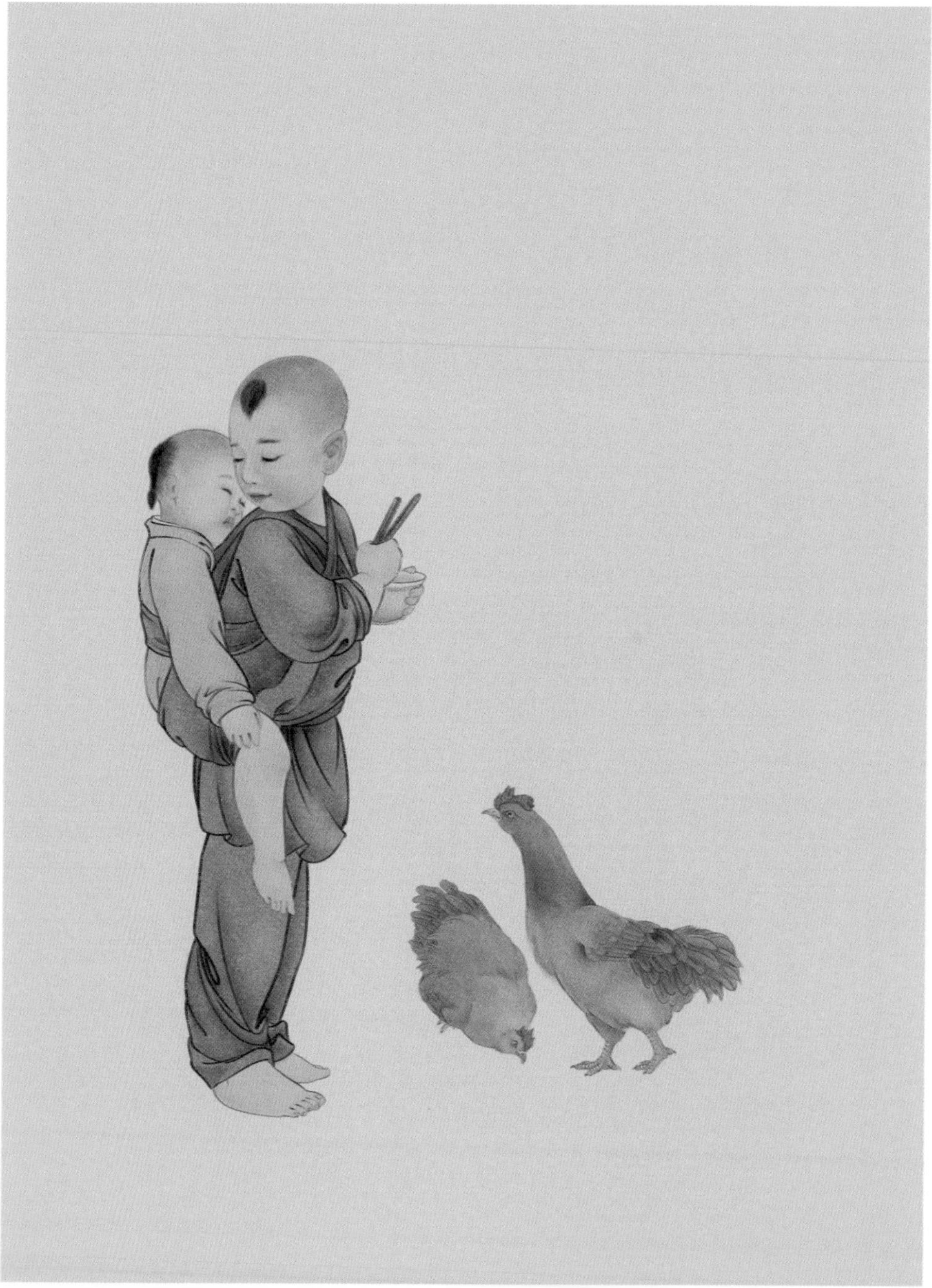

Whatever you do, ask yourself,
"Can I do it with joy in my heart?"

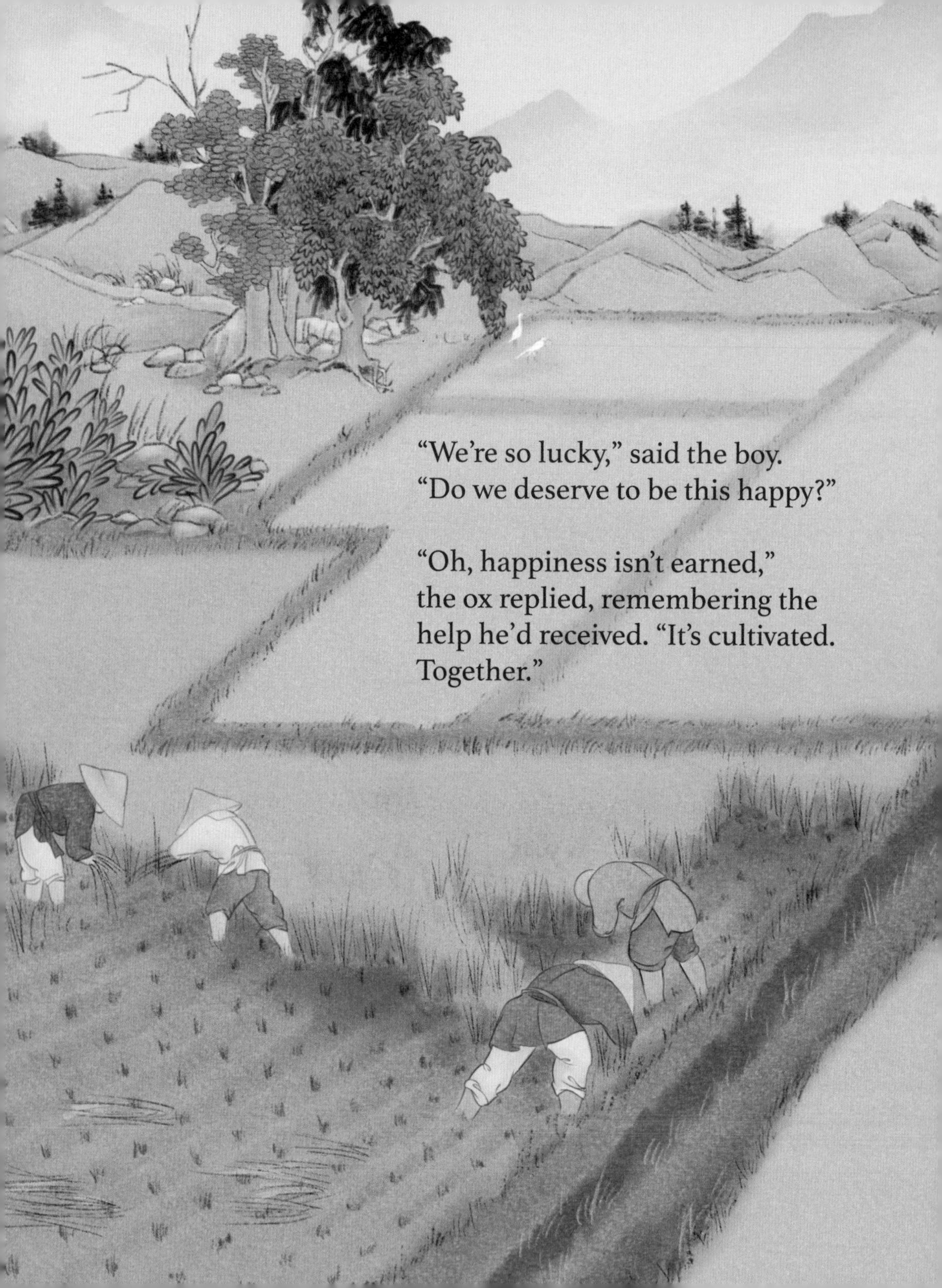

"We're so lucky," said the boy.
"Do we deserve to be this happy?"

"Oh, happiness isn't earned," the ox replied, remembering the help he'd received. "It's cultivated. Together."

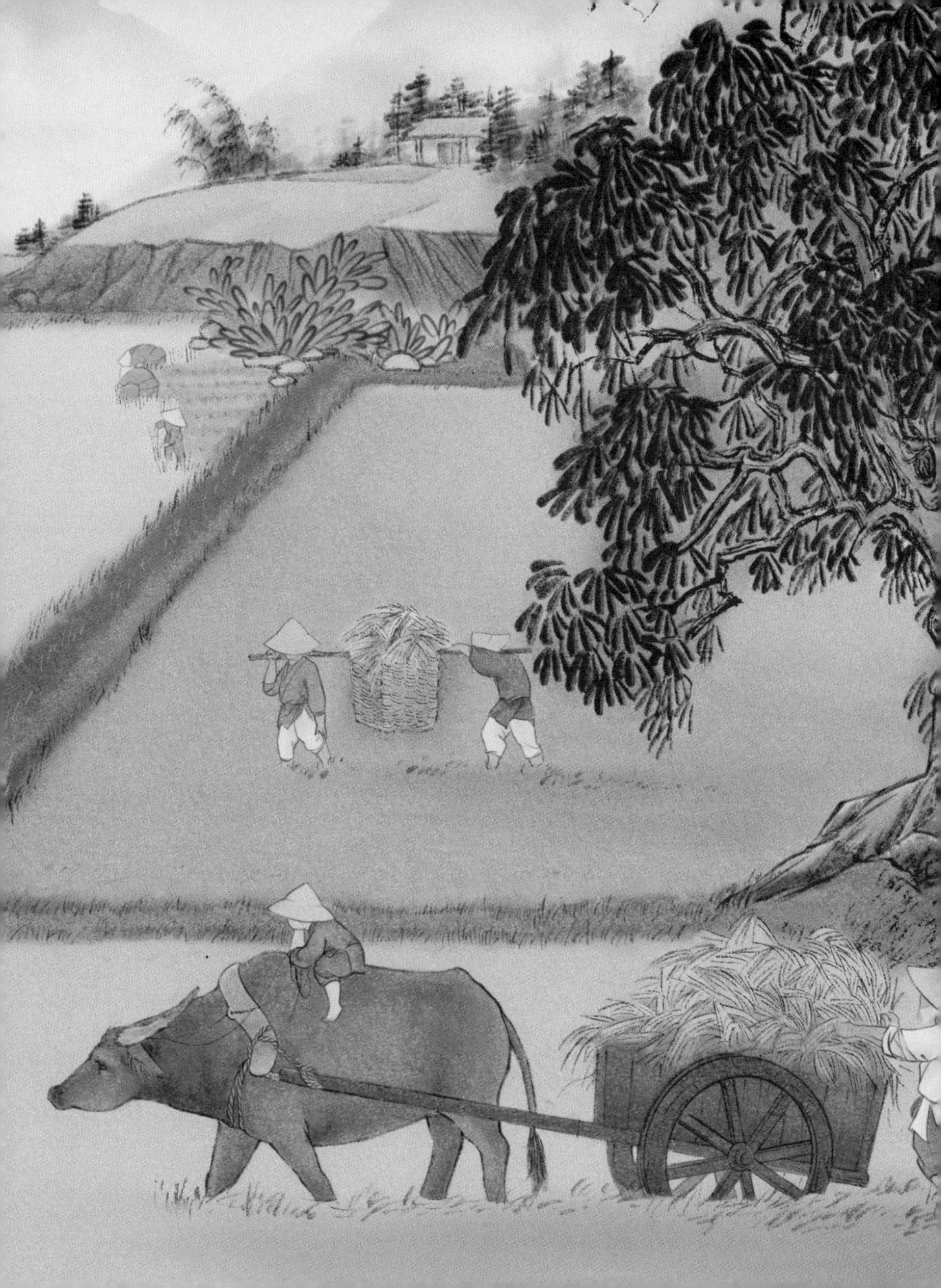

"What do you think helps
you cultivate happiness?"
asked the grandfather.

The oxherd boy answered right away. "I have the ability to hold two opposing views in my head:

One, an image of strength and power,

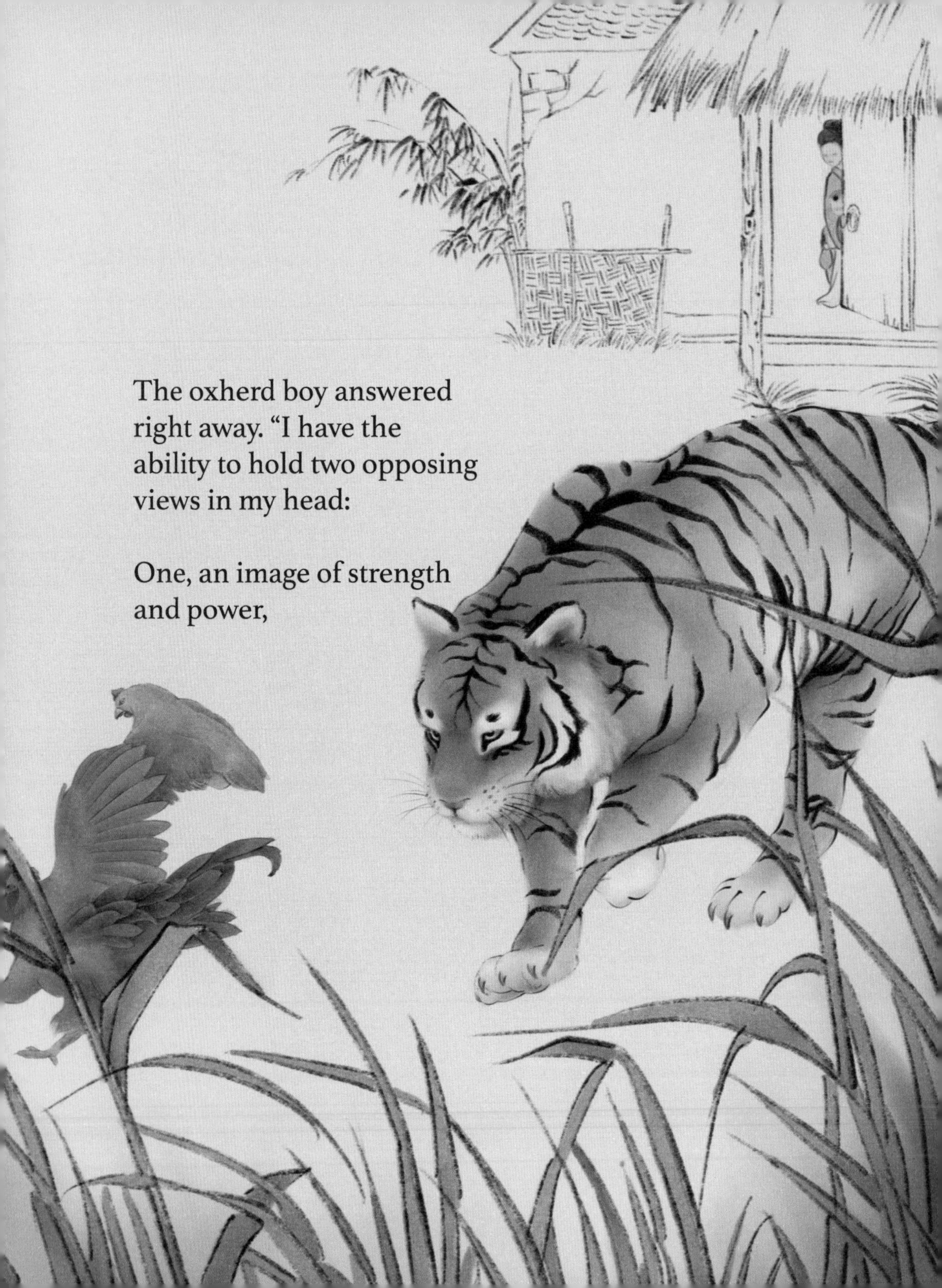

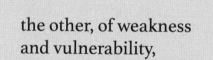

the other, of weakness
and vulnerability,

and have both be right."

"That *is* a great ability,"
his grandfather agreed,

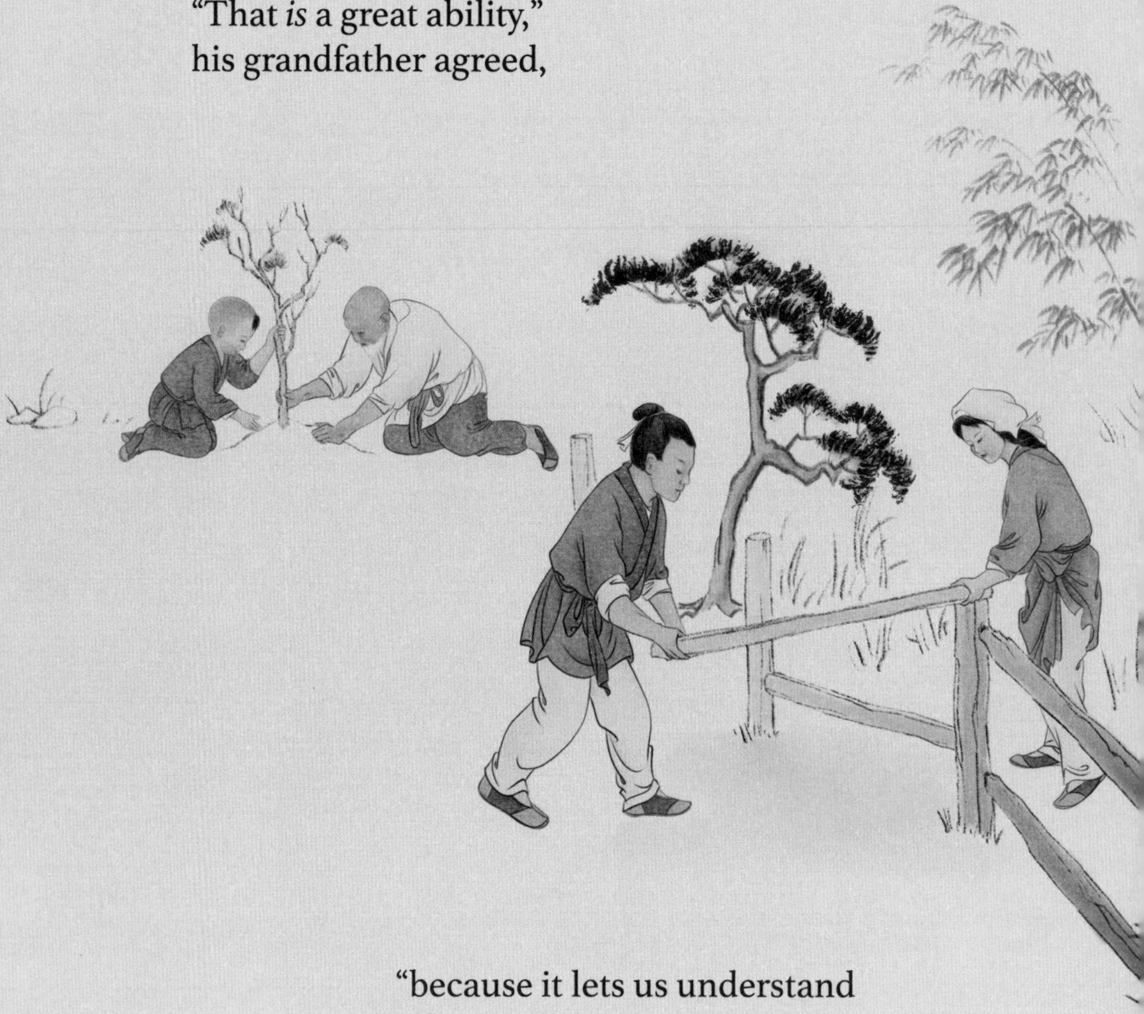

"because it lets us understand
others with compassion and
think of creative solutions . . ."

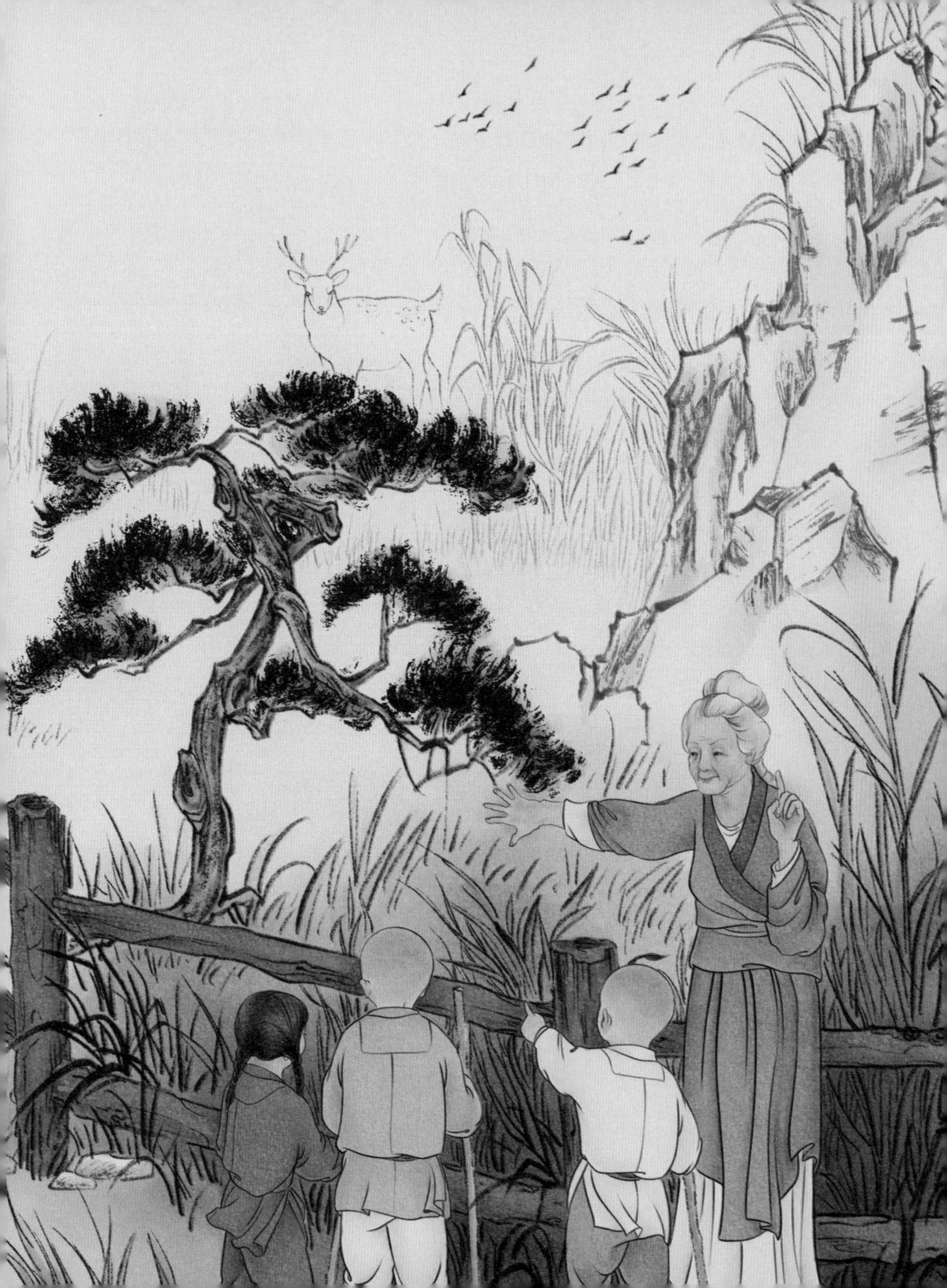

"... for the well-being
of all living things."

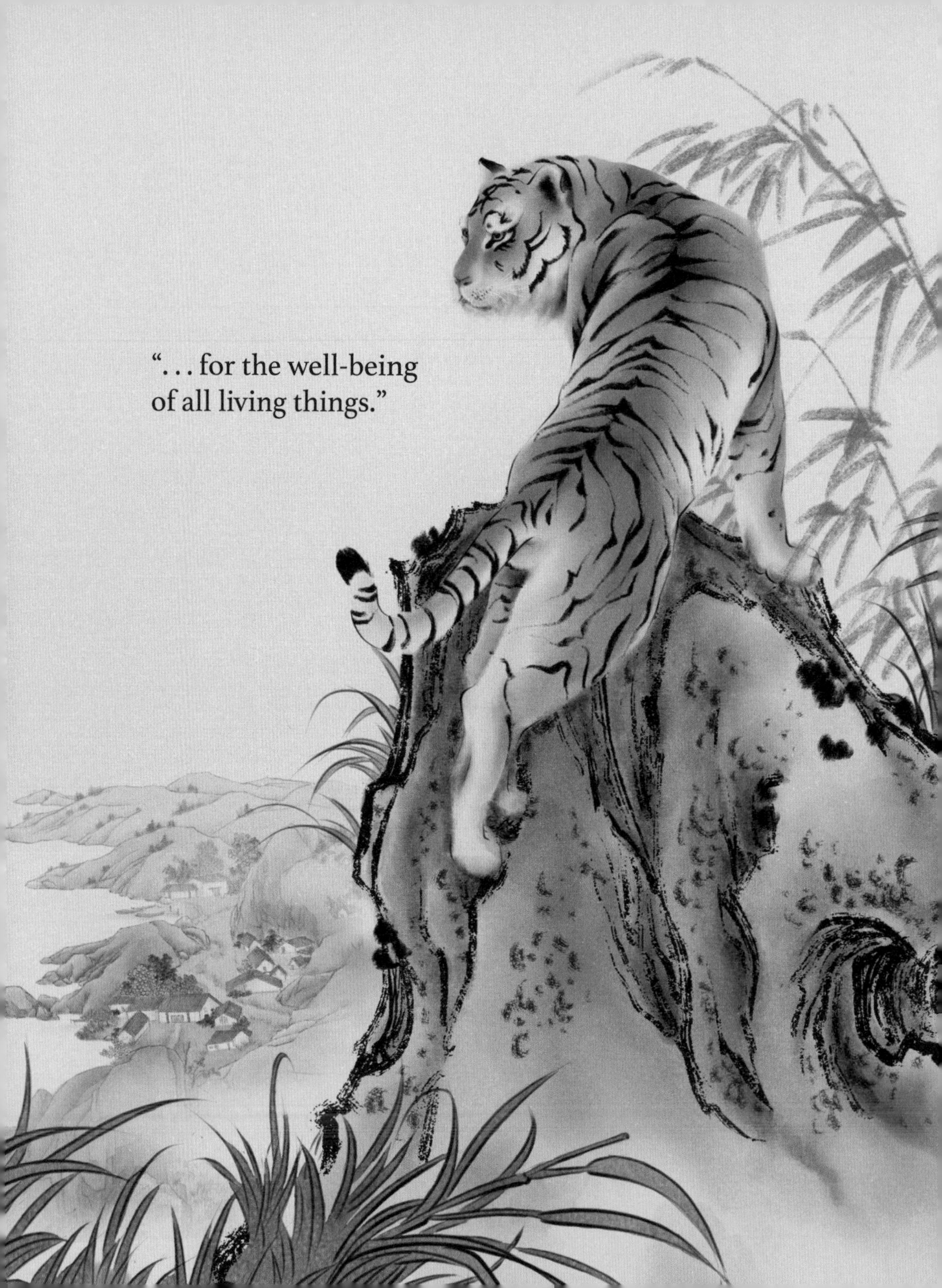

"What should we do with this ability of ours?" the boy asked his friends.

"All that we can," began the rabbit.

"In the time that we have," finished the ox.

“There are songs inside me that no one can play but myself. Whether others listen or not, I’m still responsible for the music I make.”

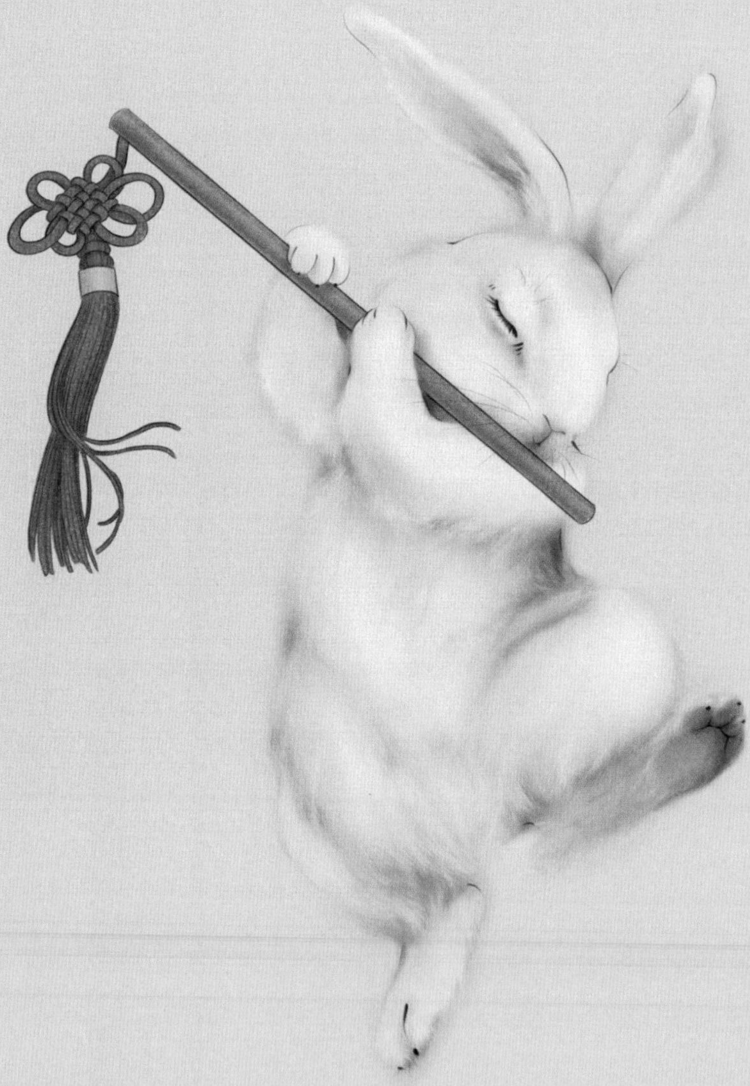

The boy listened, enraptured,
as the rabbit finished her song.
"How do you make such a
unique sound?" he asked.

"I simply play who I am.
The secret," she replied with
a wink, "is that I'm always
changing."

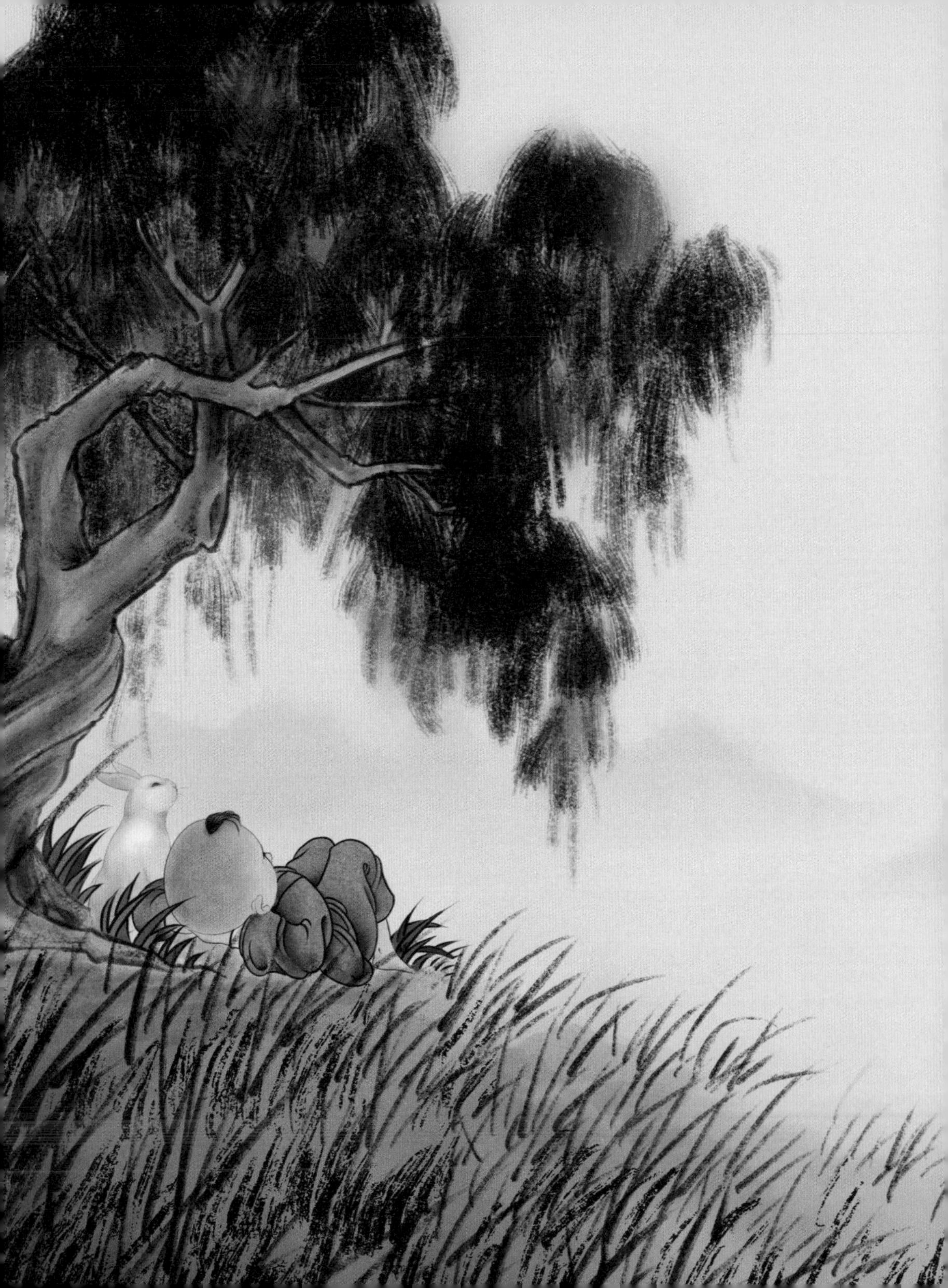

The rabbit couldn't sit still. "Don't you think that we're wasting time?"

"Yes," the oxherd boy replied slowly, "but wasting time with you is exactly what makes you special to me."

"Oh, then maybe it's not wasted after all."

What's important is not
how much we do, but how
much we love. So let's do
what inspires us to love.

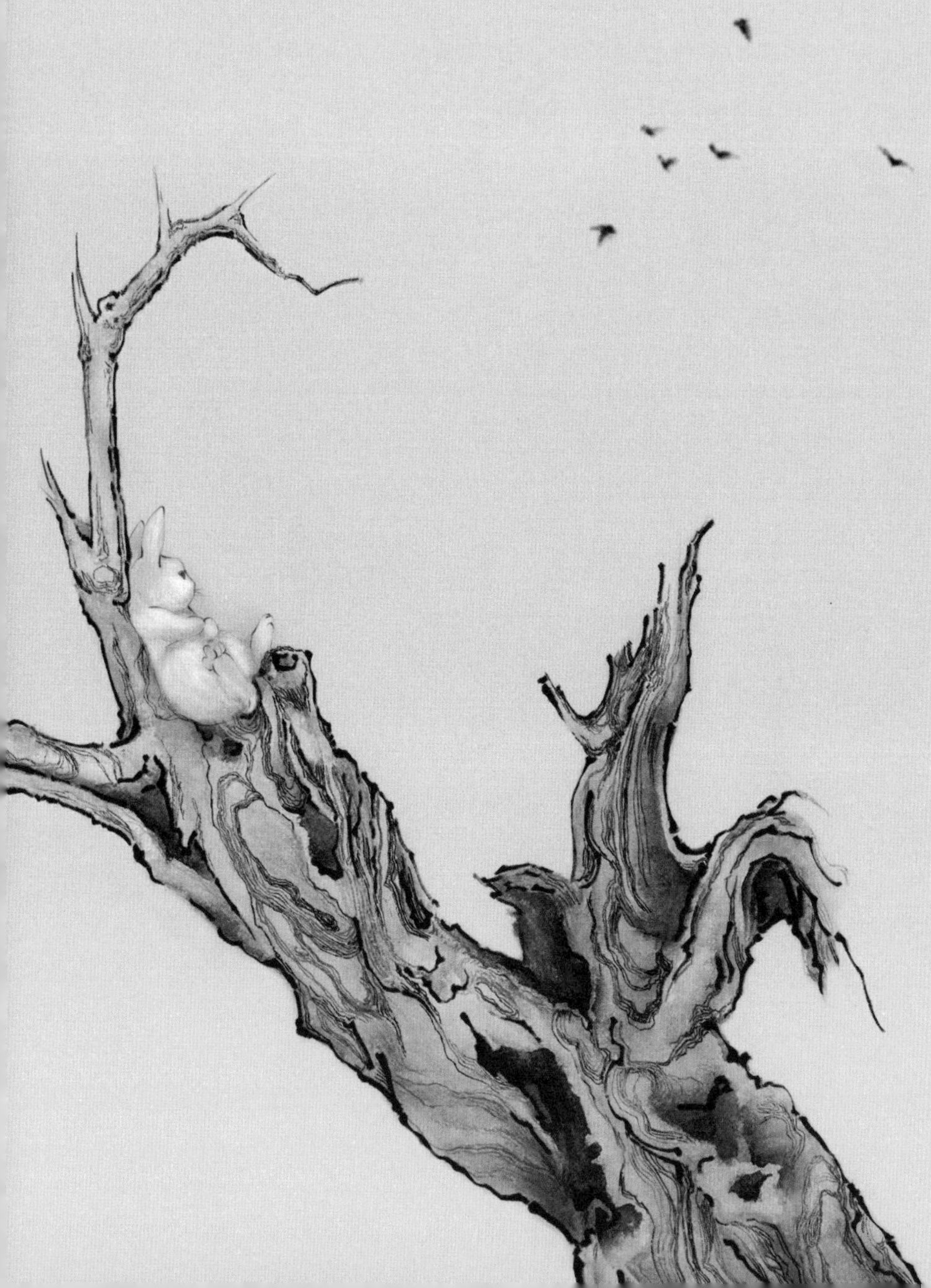

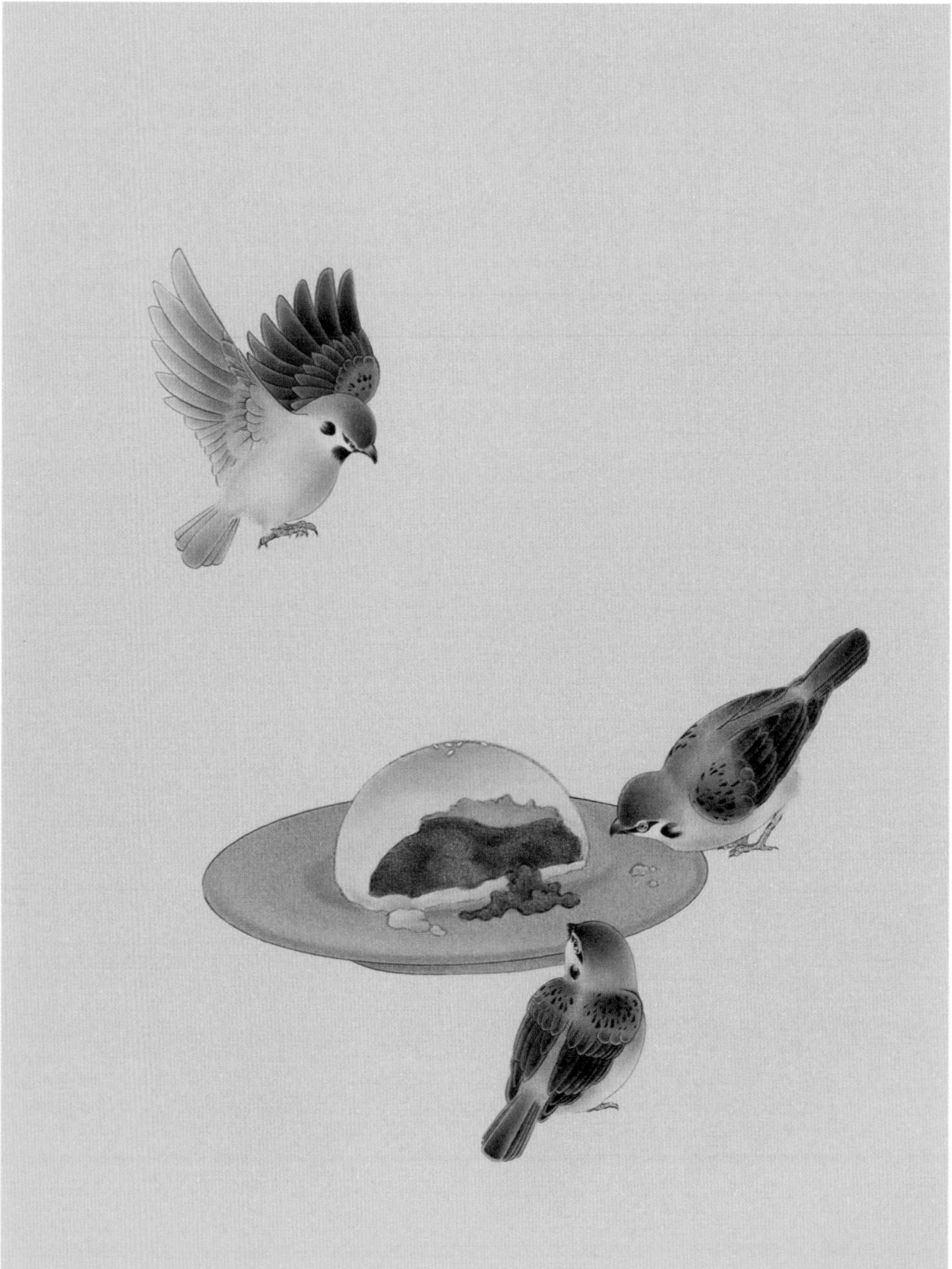

Love began to look different to the grandfather. “I should think I’m old enough to put on my own shoes,” he mused.

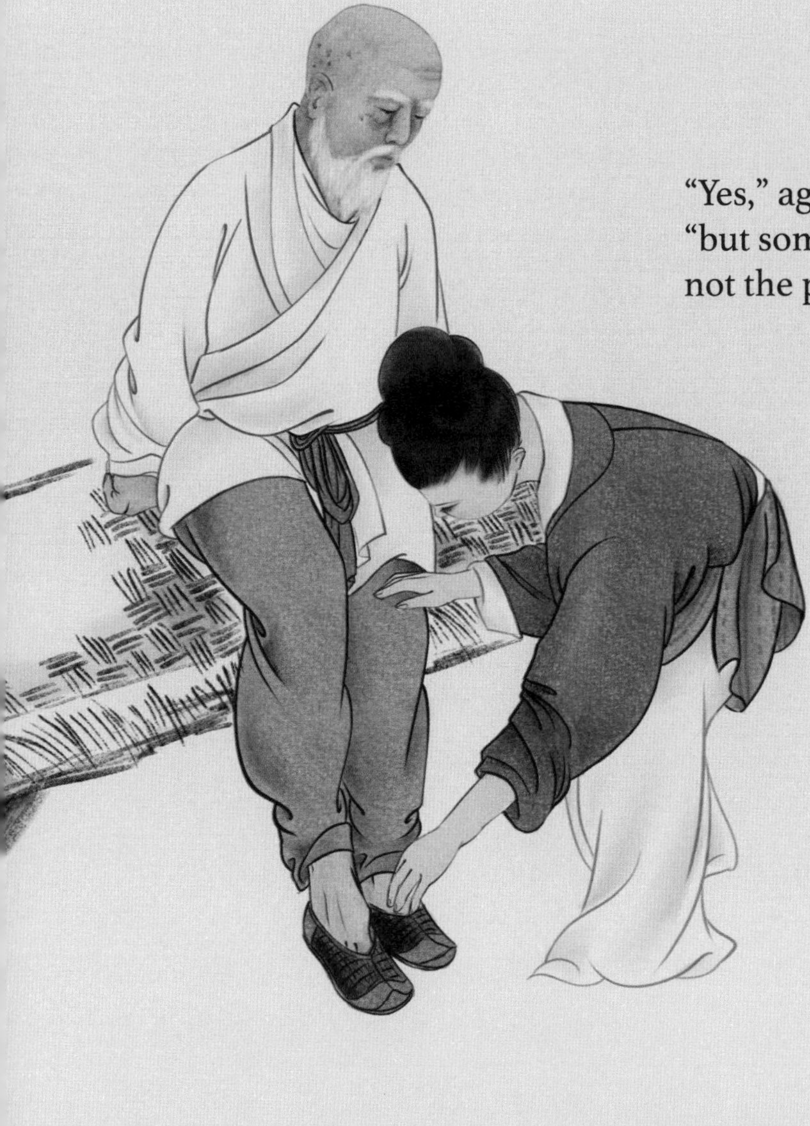

“Yes,” agreed his niece, “but sometimes that’s not the point.”

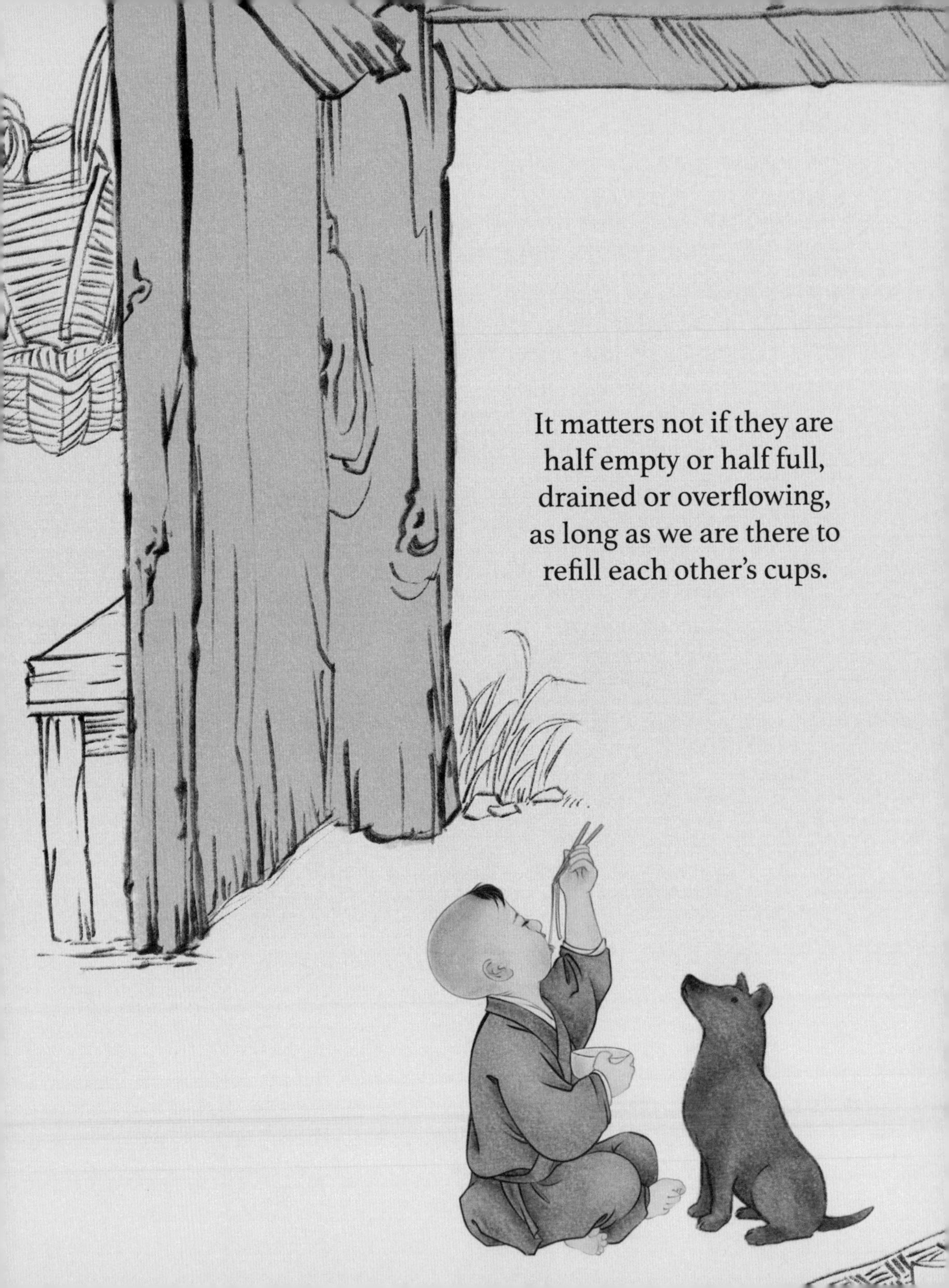

It matters not if they are
half empty or half full,
drained or overflowing,
as long as we are there to
refill each other's cups.

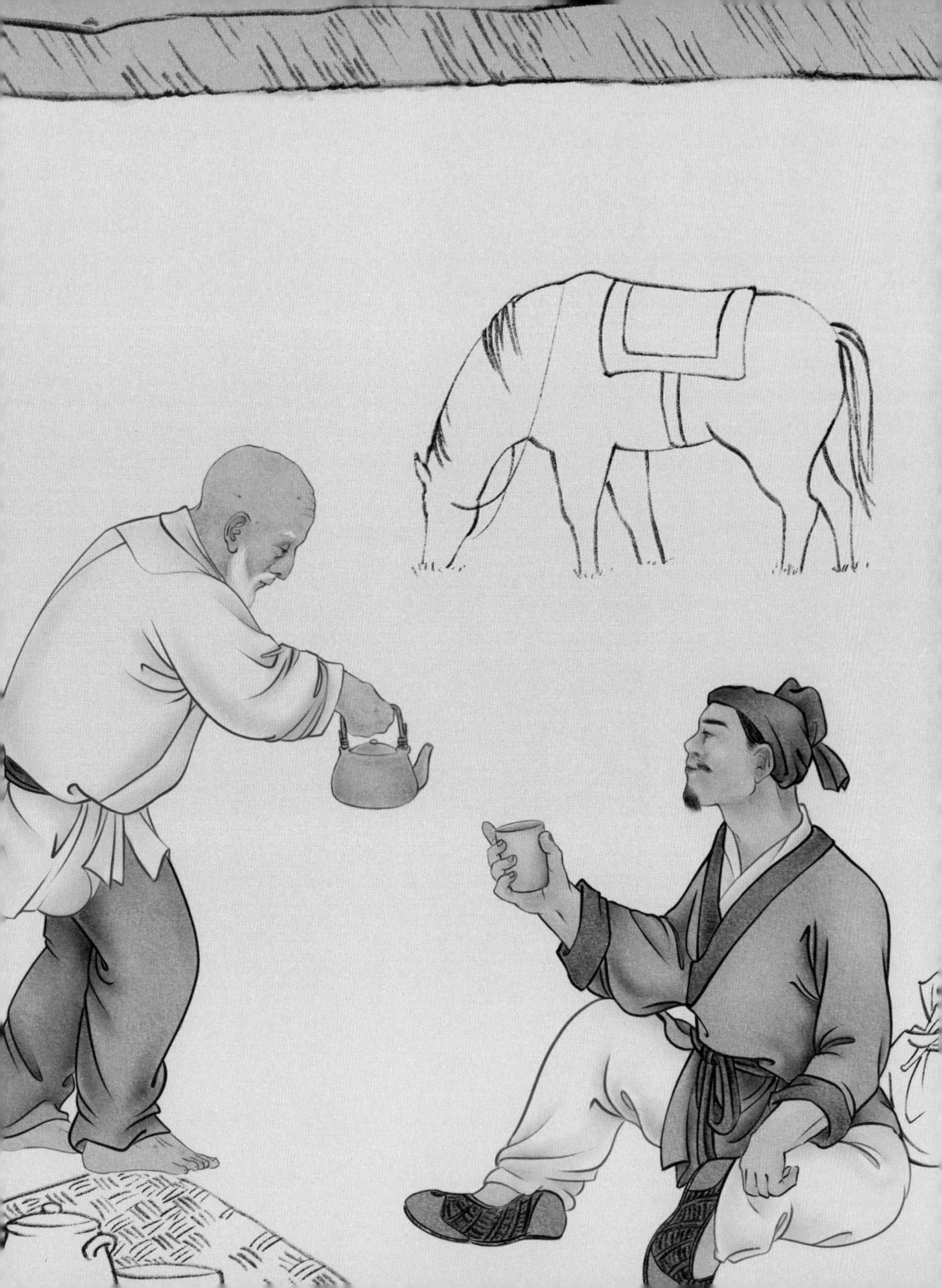

"Being with you has been the greatest privilege of my life," murmured the grandfather.

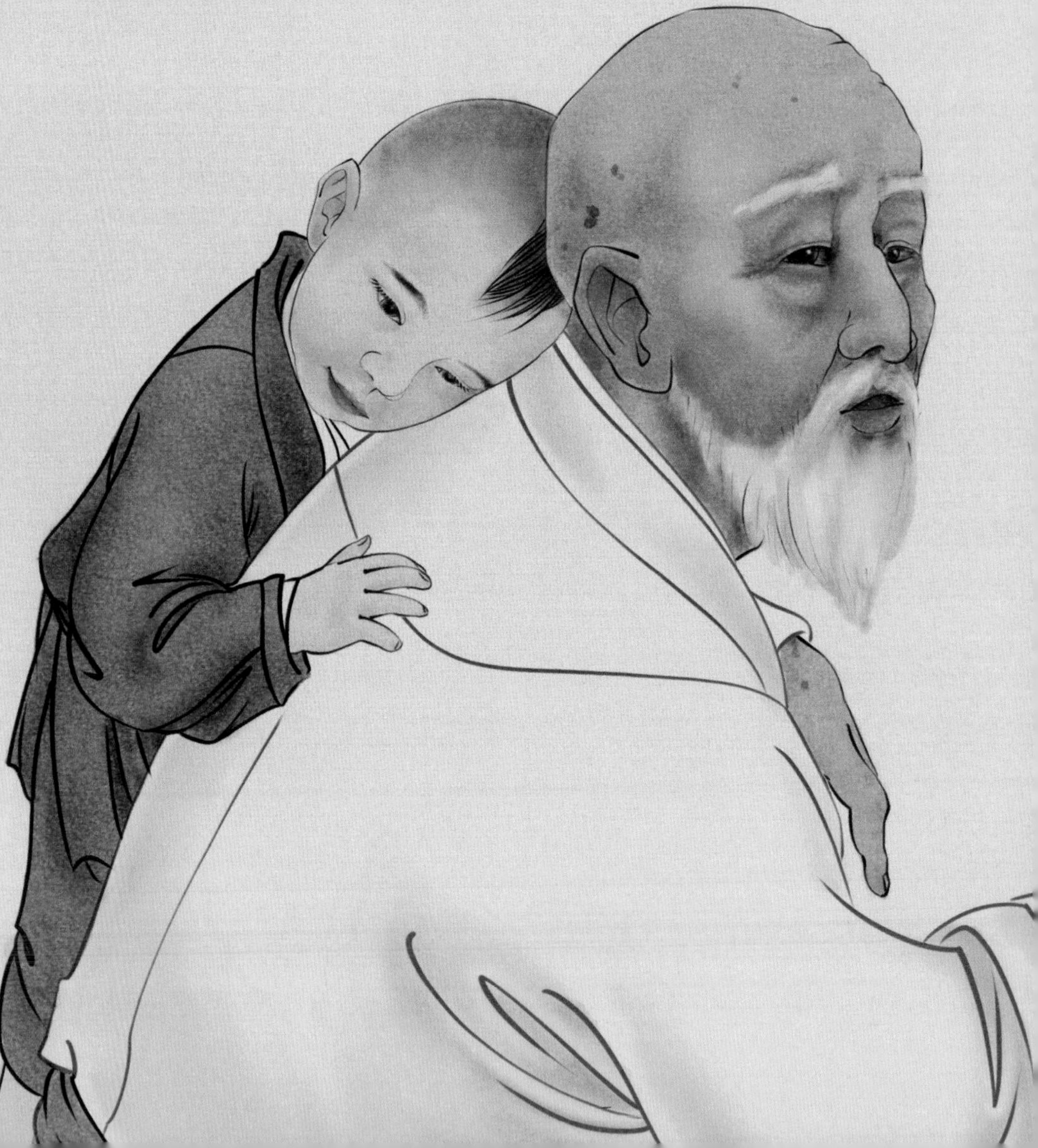

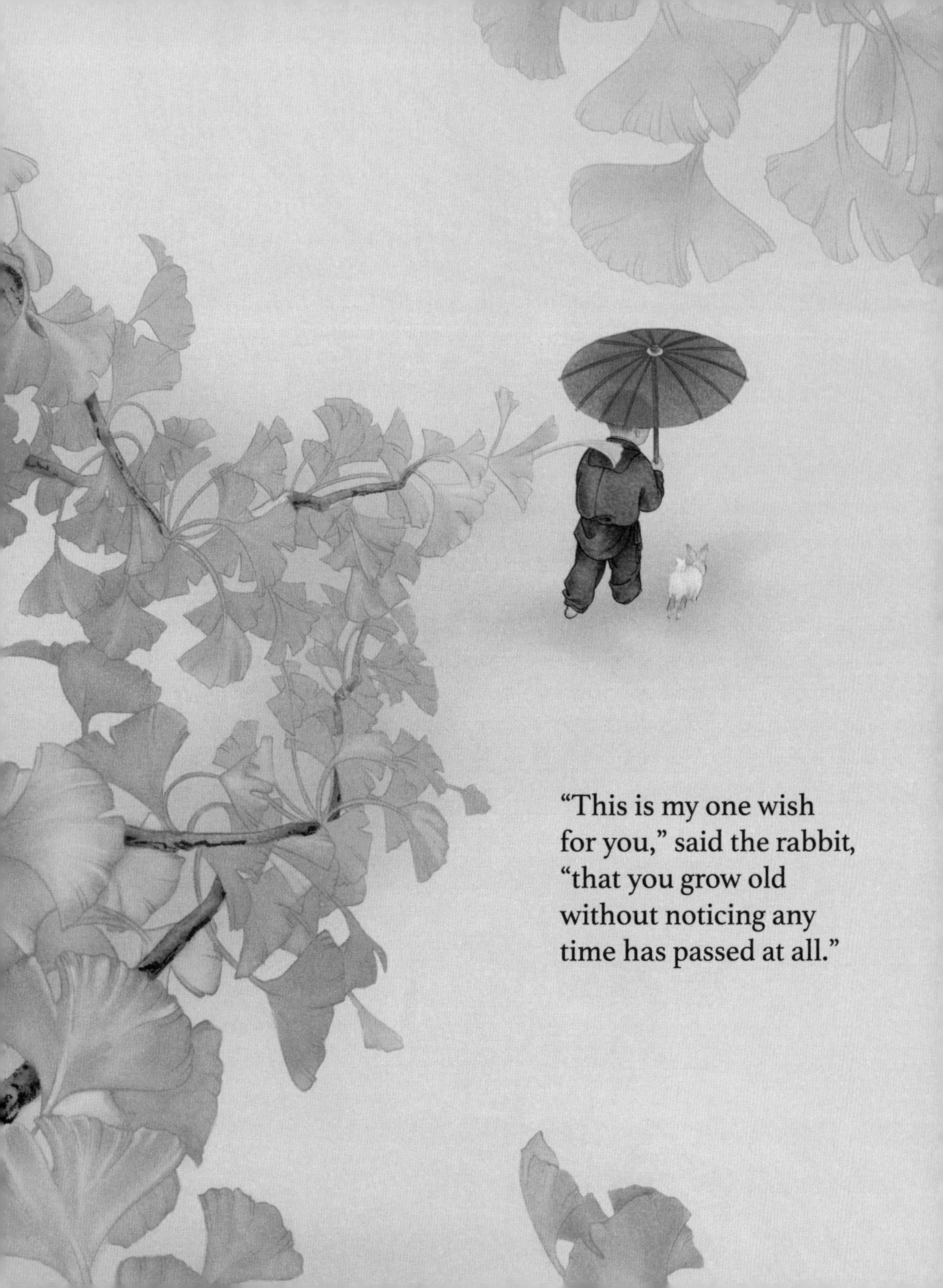

"This is my one wish
for you," said the rabbit,
"that you grow old
without noticing any
time has passed at all."

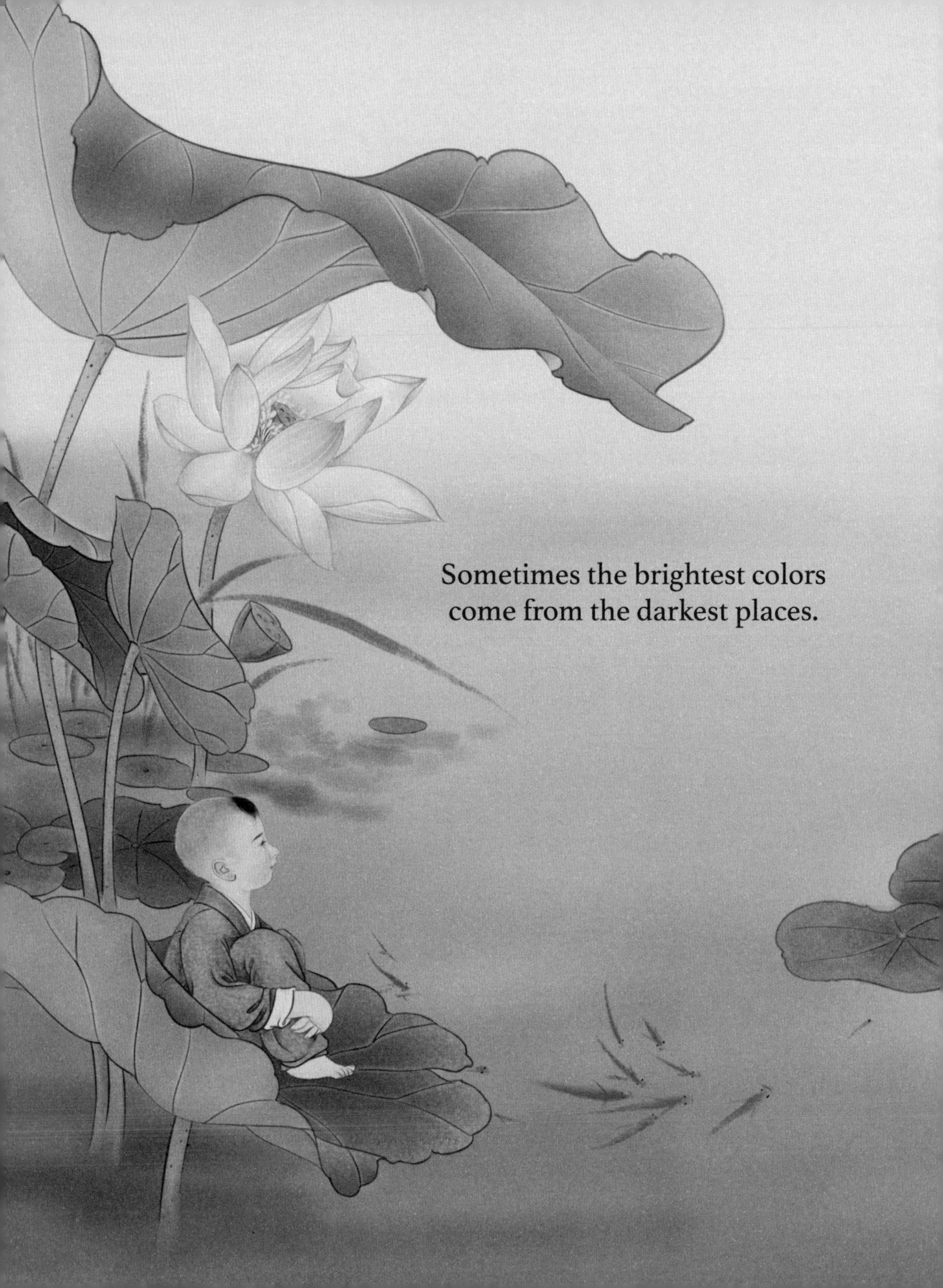

Sometimes the brightest colors
come from the darkest places.

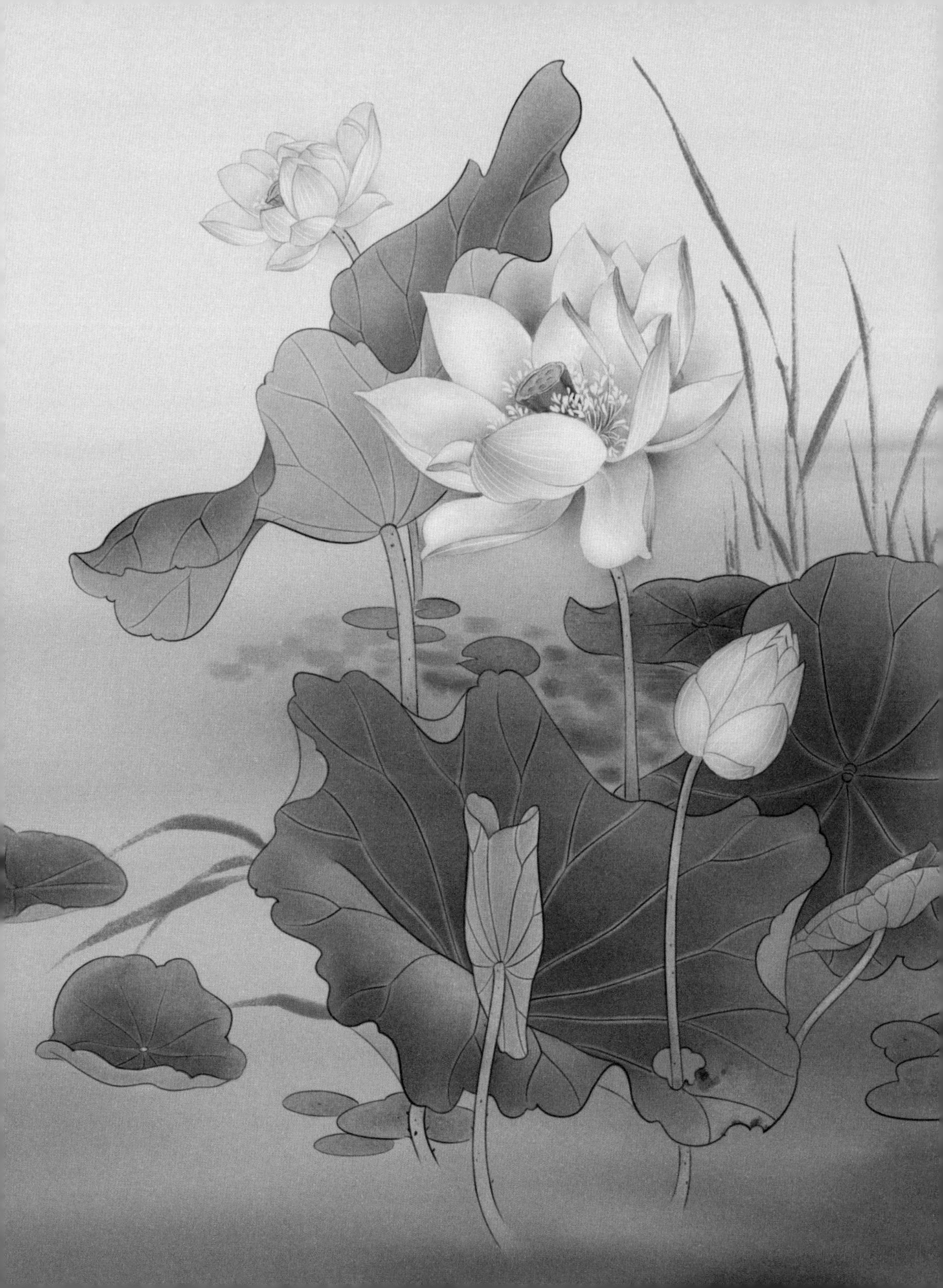

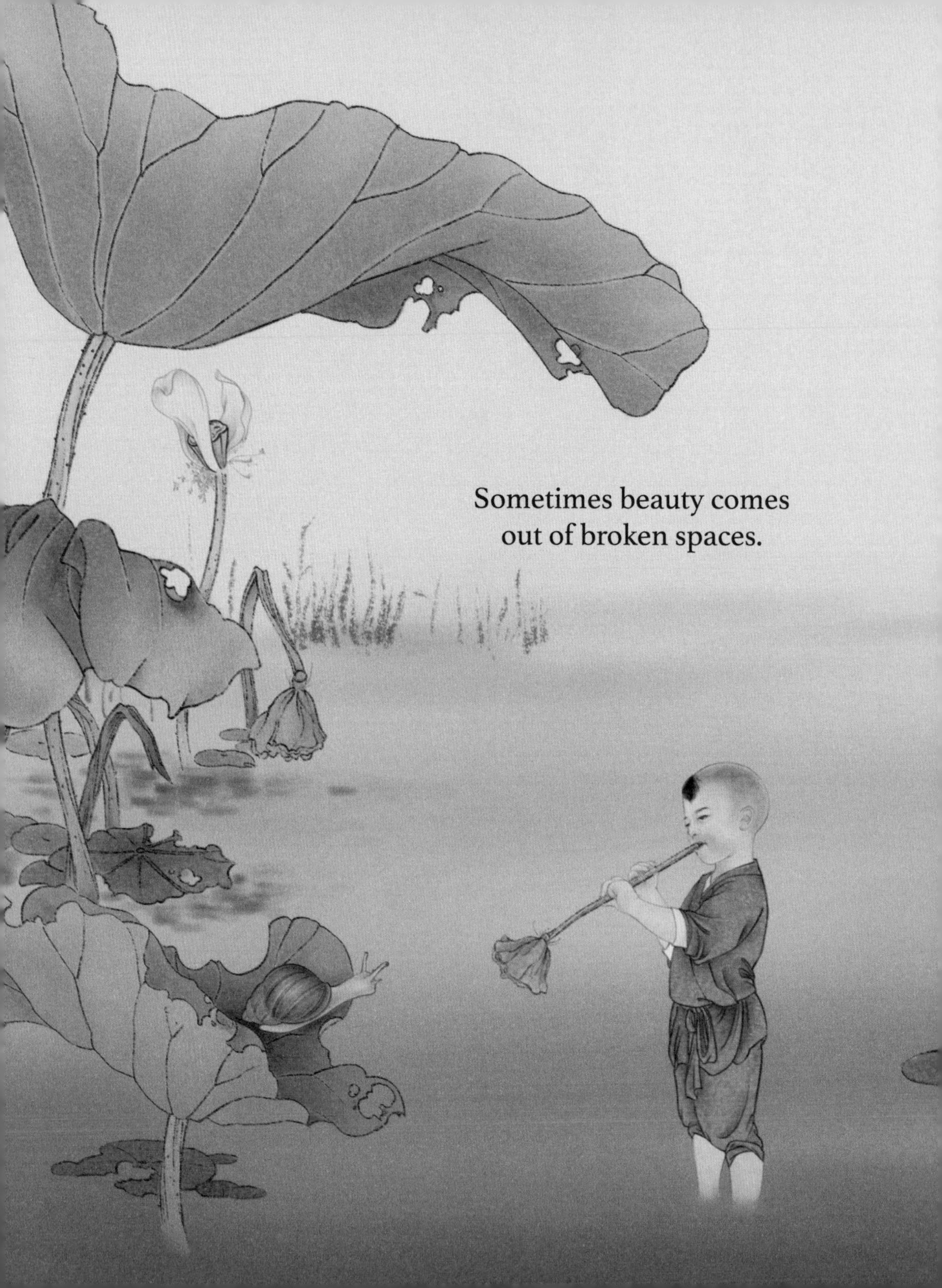

Sometimes beauty comes
out of broken spaces.

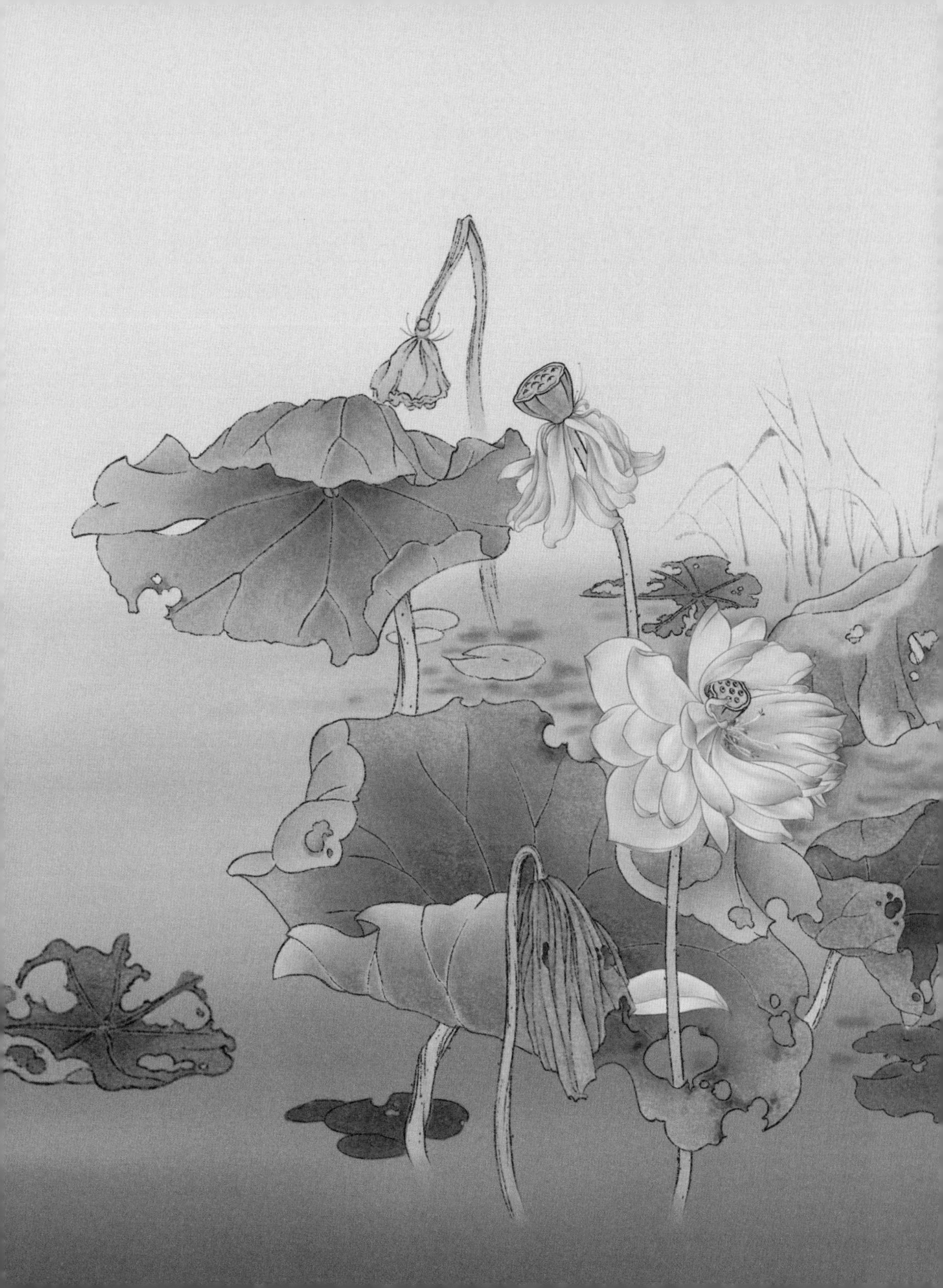

"Do you think flowers are ever ready to die?" asked the rabbit.

"Maybe they're more concerned about living a full life," the ox replied.

The boy nodded. "I guess it's the same thing."

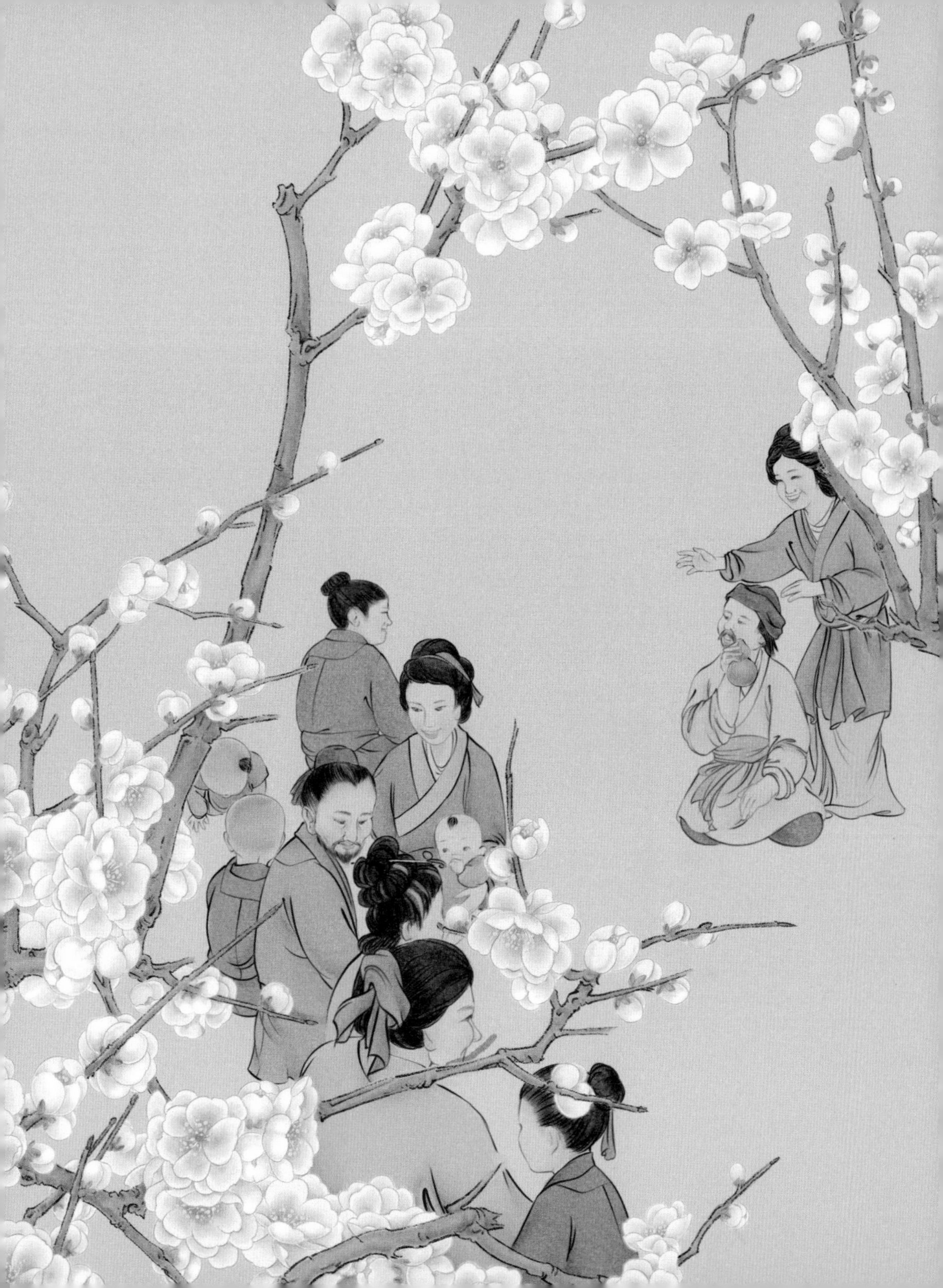

“What do you think happens when we die?” asked the oxherd boy.

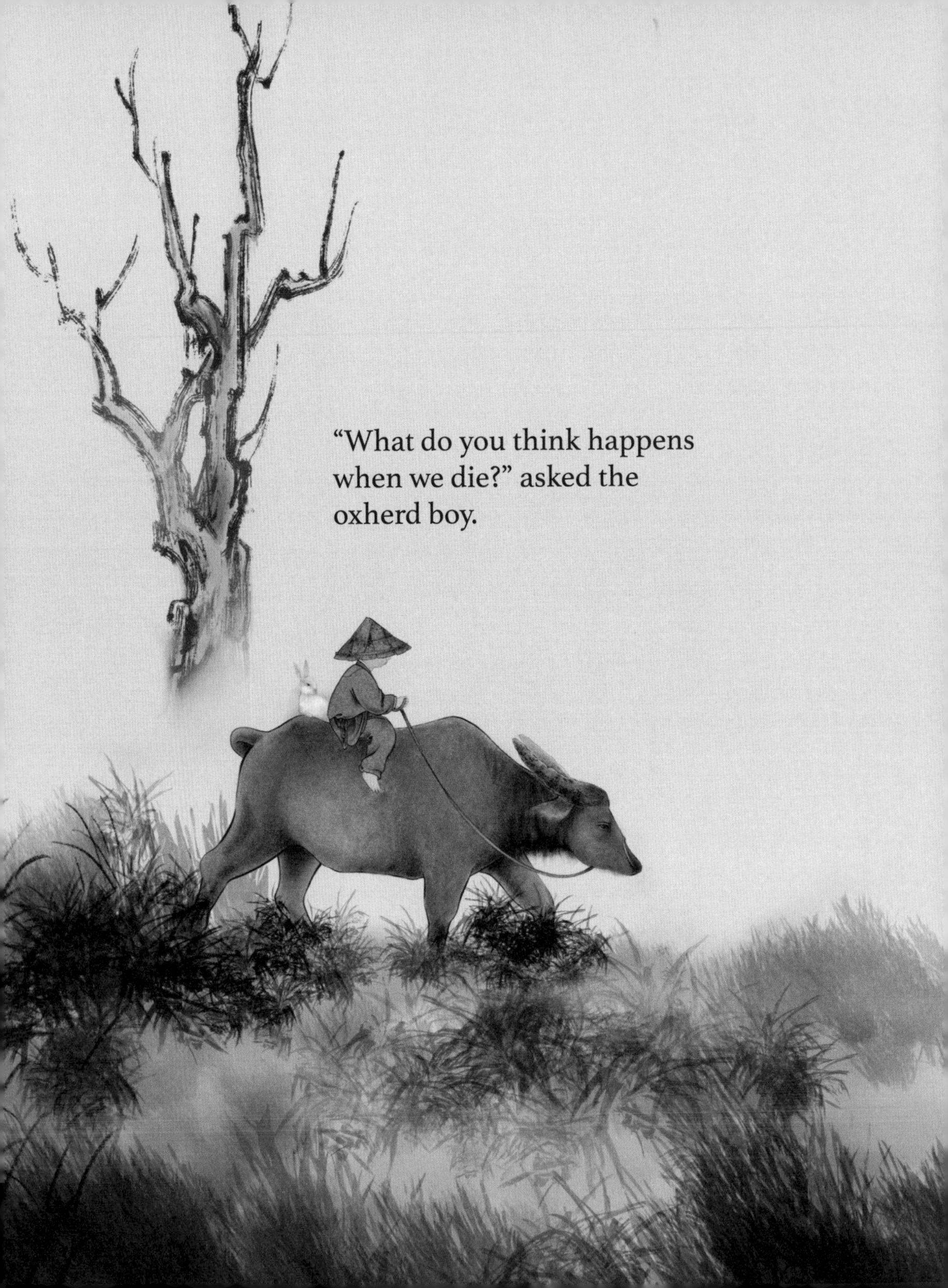

"Well, what happens when we are born?" the ox asked in return.

"We don't arrive into this world separate and whole. We emerge like waves from the sea.

Maybe dying is like a wave falling back to the ocean . . ."

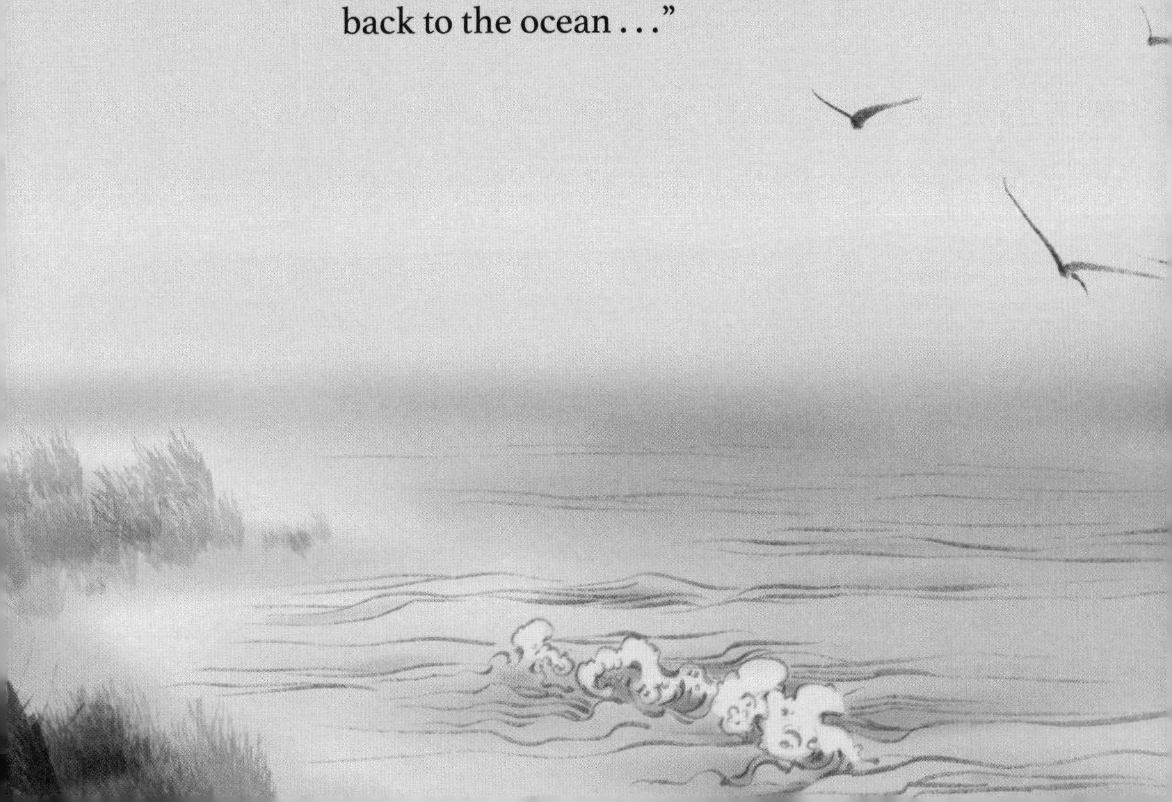

"... a return to the same vast home
to which we belong with all things."

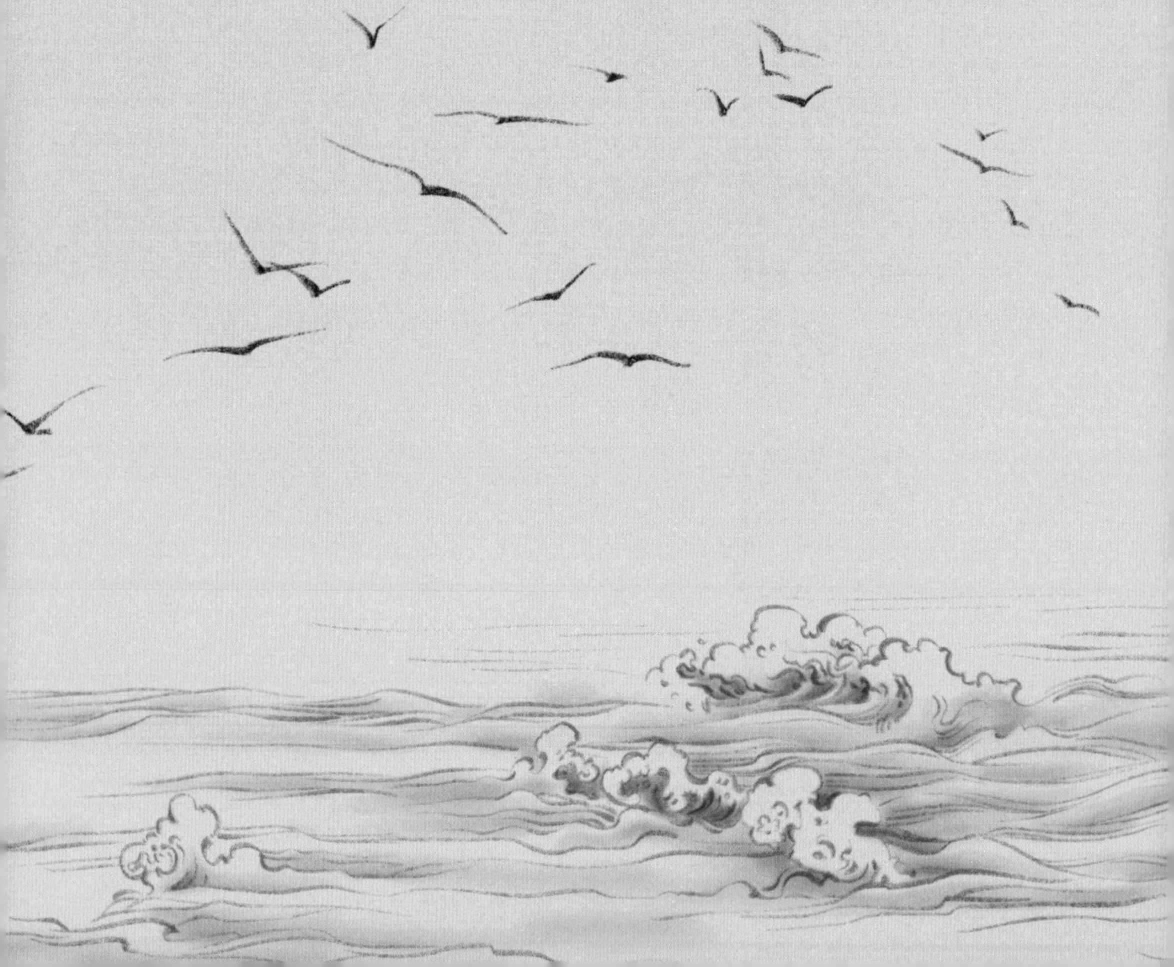

“Does that mean you
wouldn’t miss me?”

The ox laughed.
“Of course I would.”

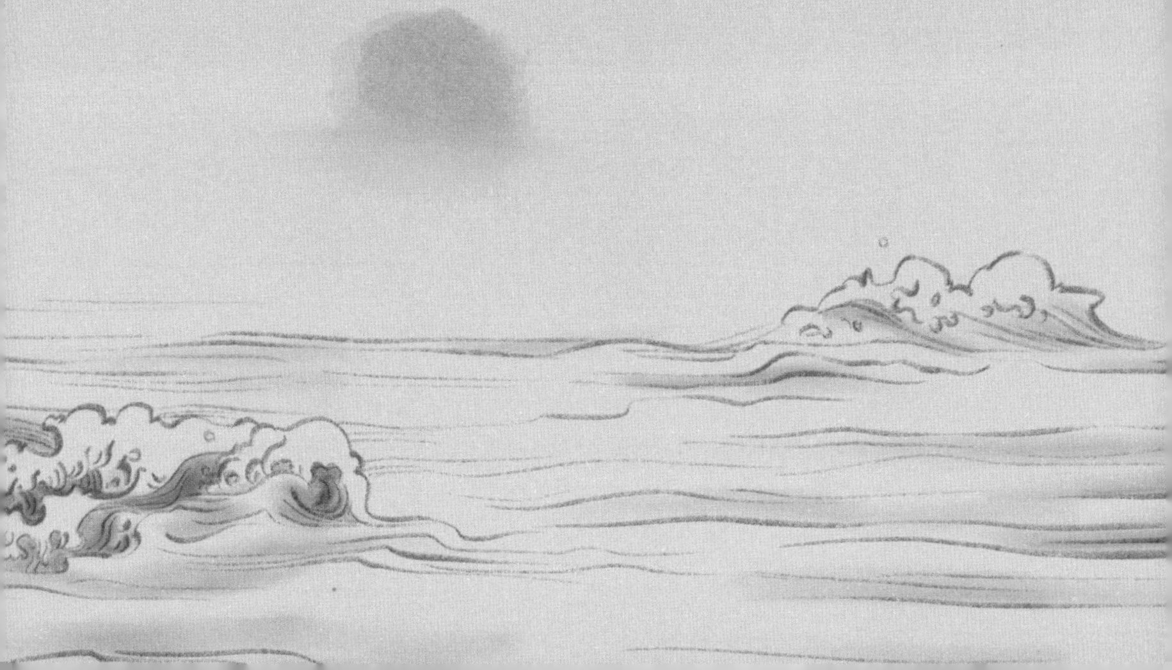

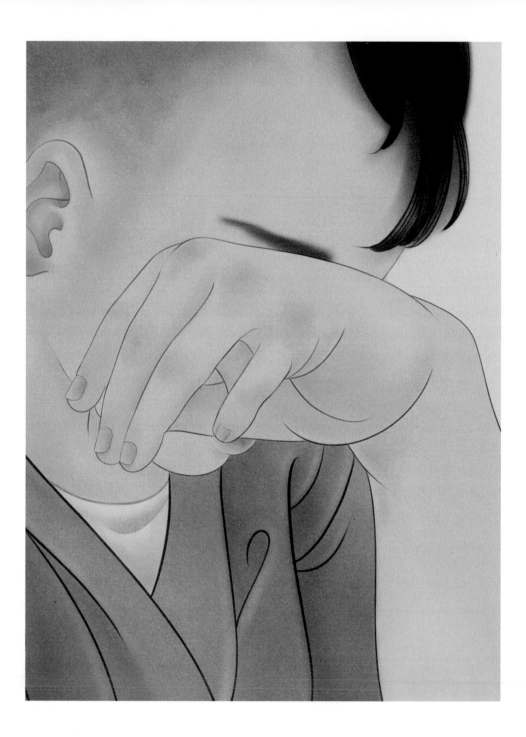

"Father said I shouldn't cry."

"Whether you cry or not, you must still hold your grief," the ox advised. "Swim in your sorrow. Let it wash over you and carry away your feelings of loss."

The oxherd boy sniffled. "What happens if I don't?" he asked.

"Your sadness will still leave you, but it will leave as anger instead."

In those quiet moments,
when all light has fled,
may you be ever so brave,
ever so tender,
ever so still.

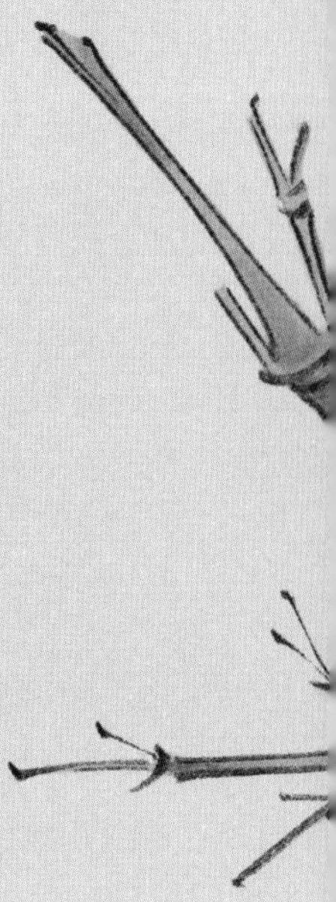

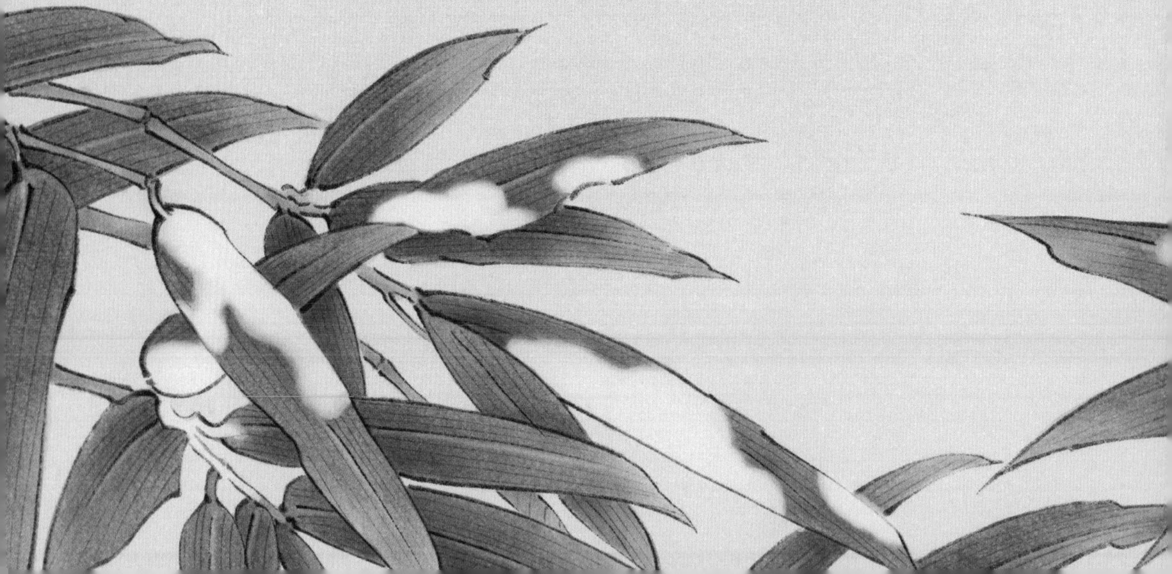

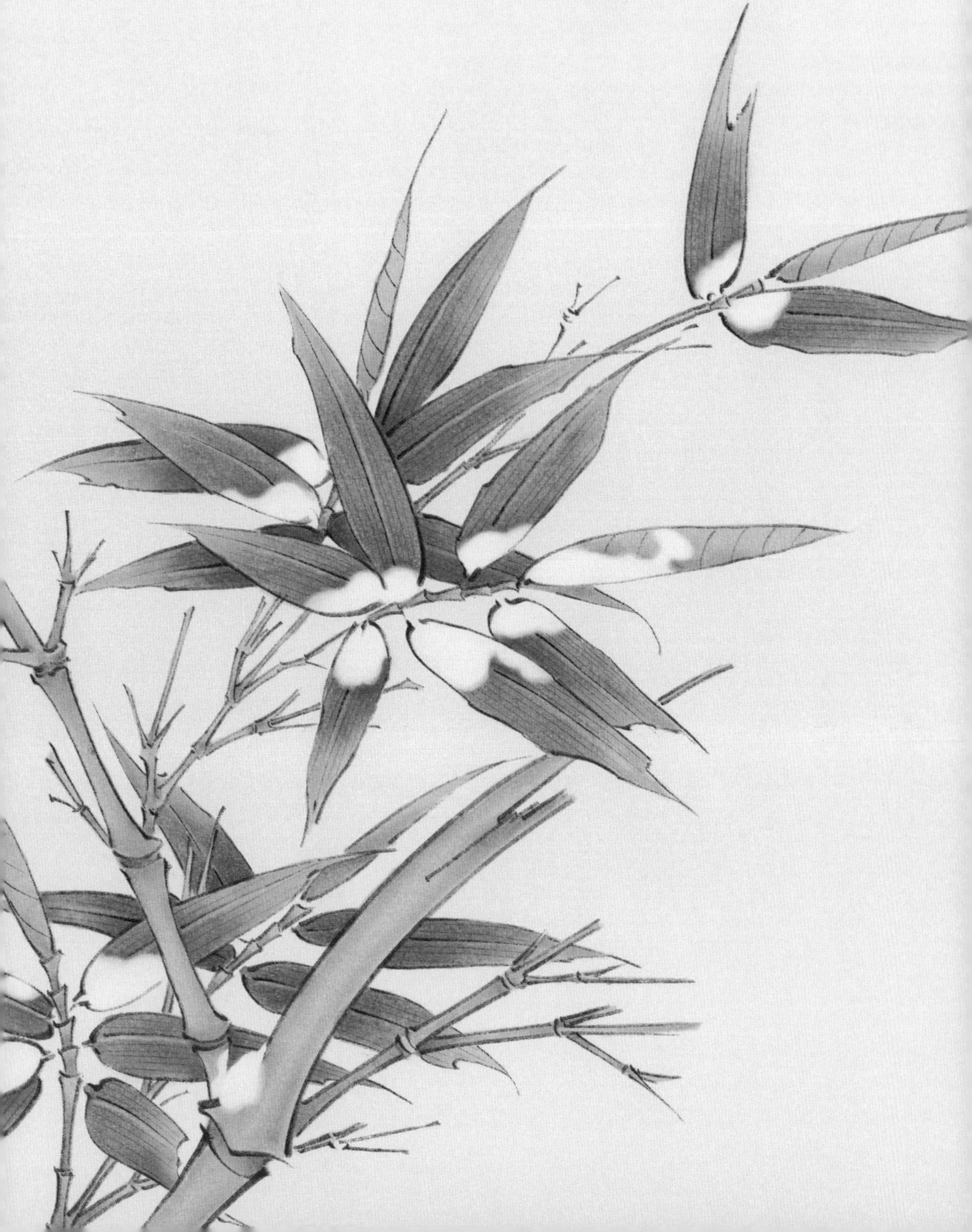

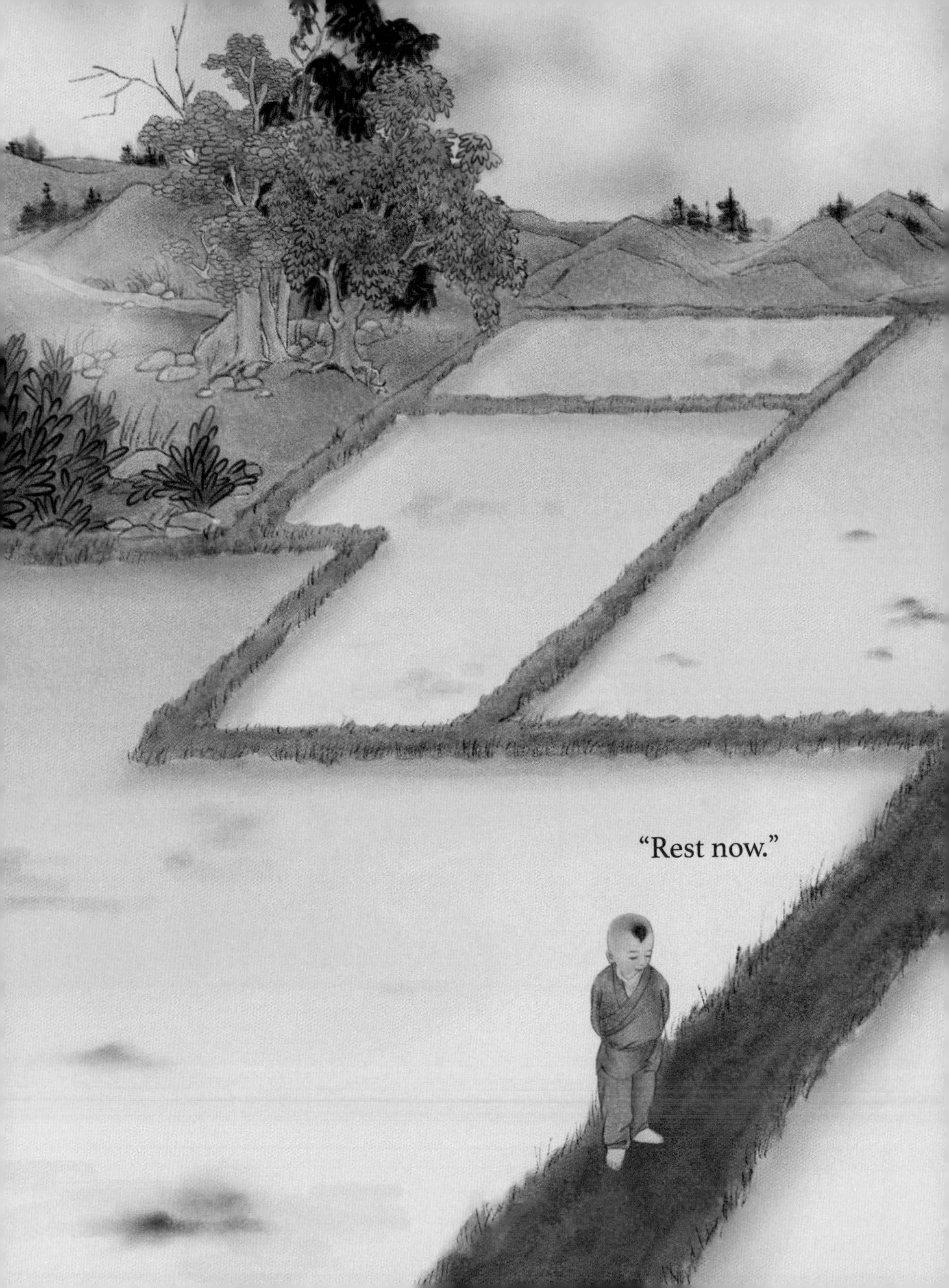

“Rest now.”

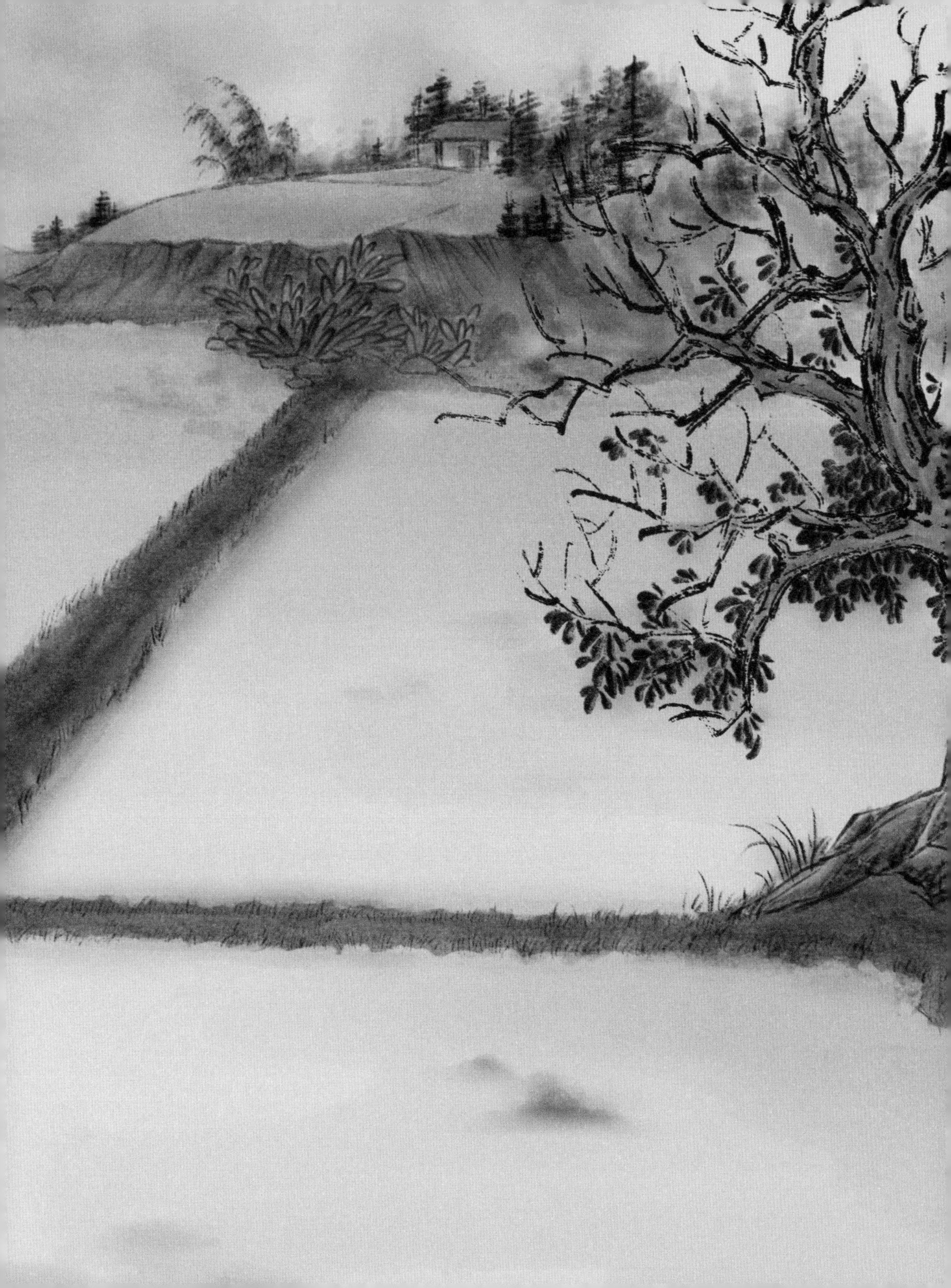

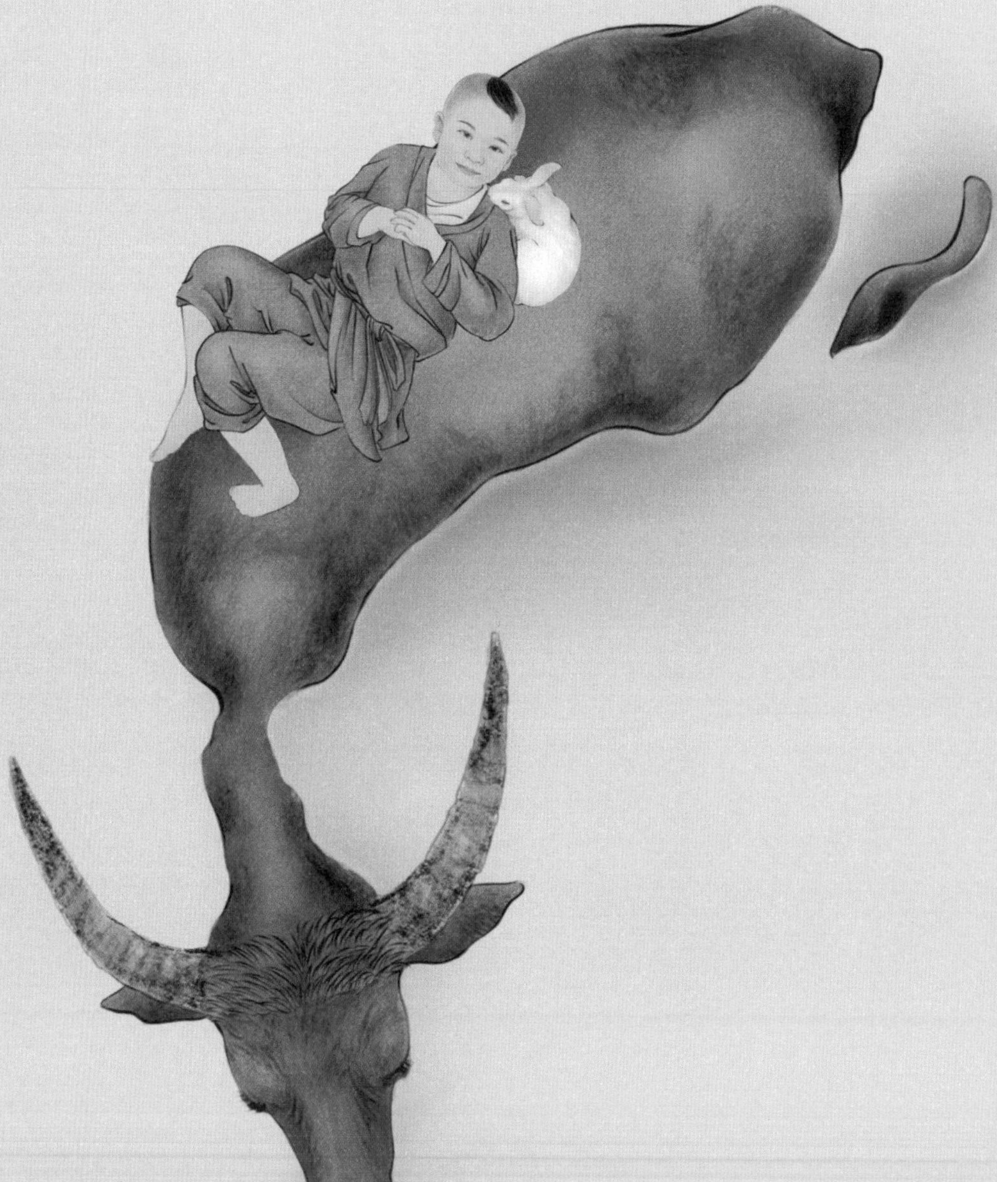

As the sun slipped behind the mountains, the boy studied the vast, empty sky above. "I wonder if there's anyone up there watching over us?"

"If there is," replied the rabbit, "I think they'd like to see us watching over one another down here, too."

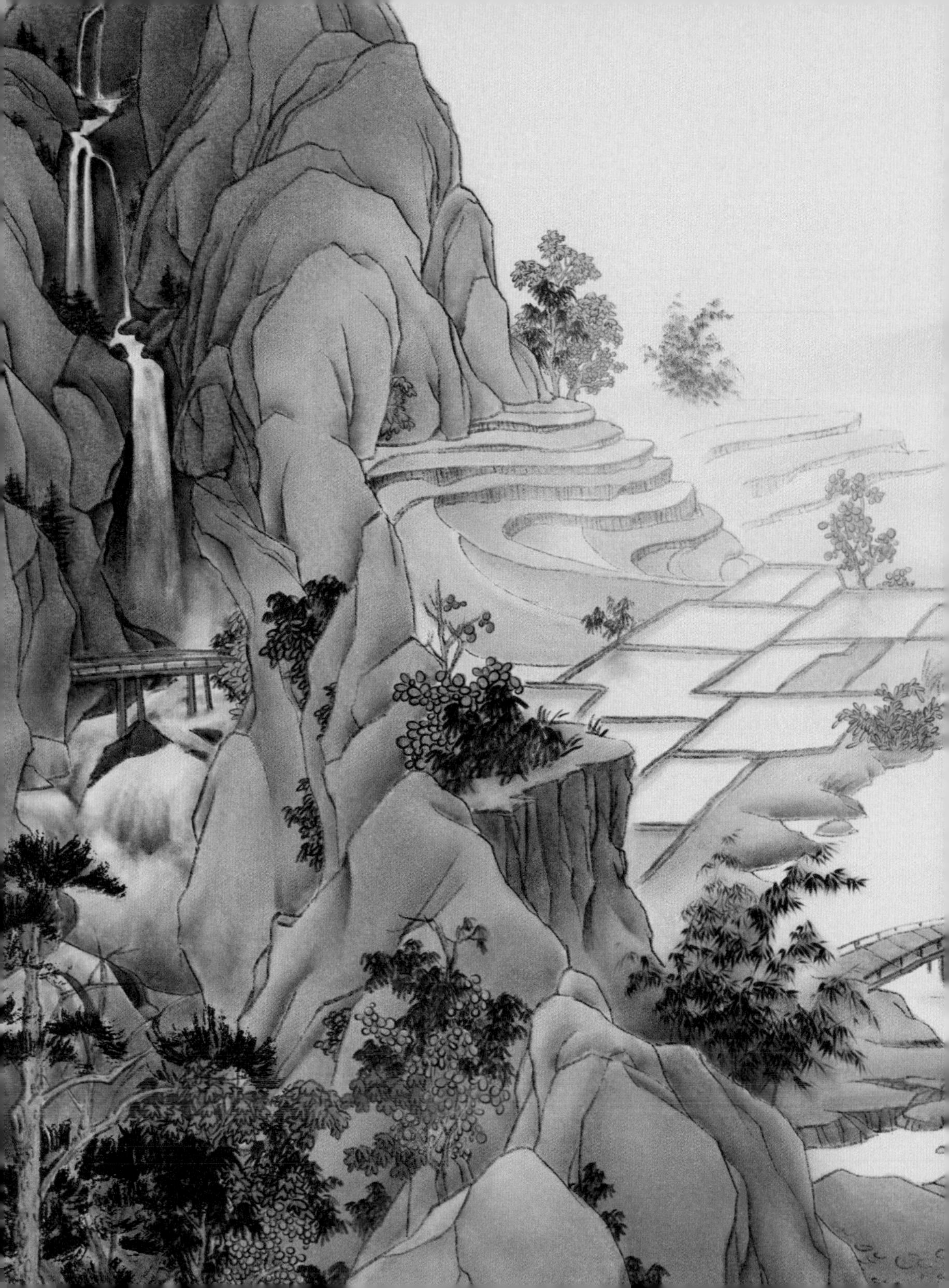

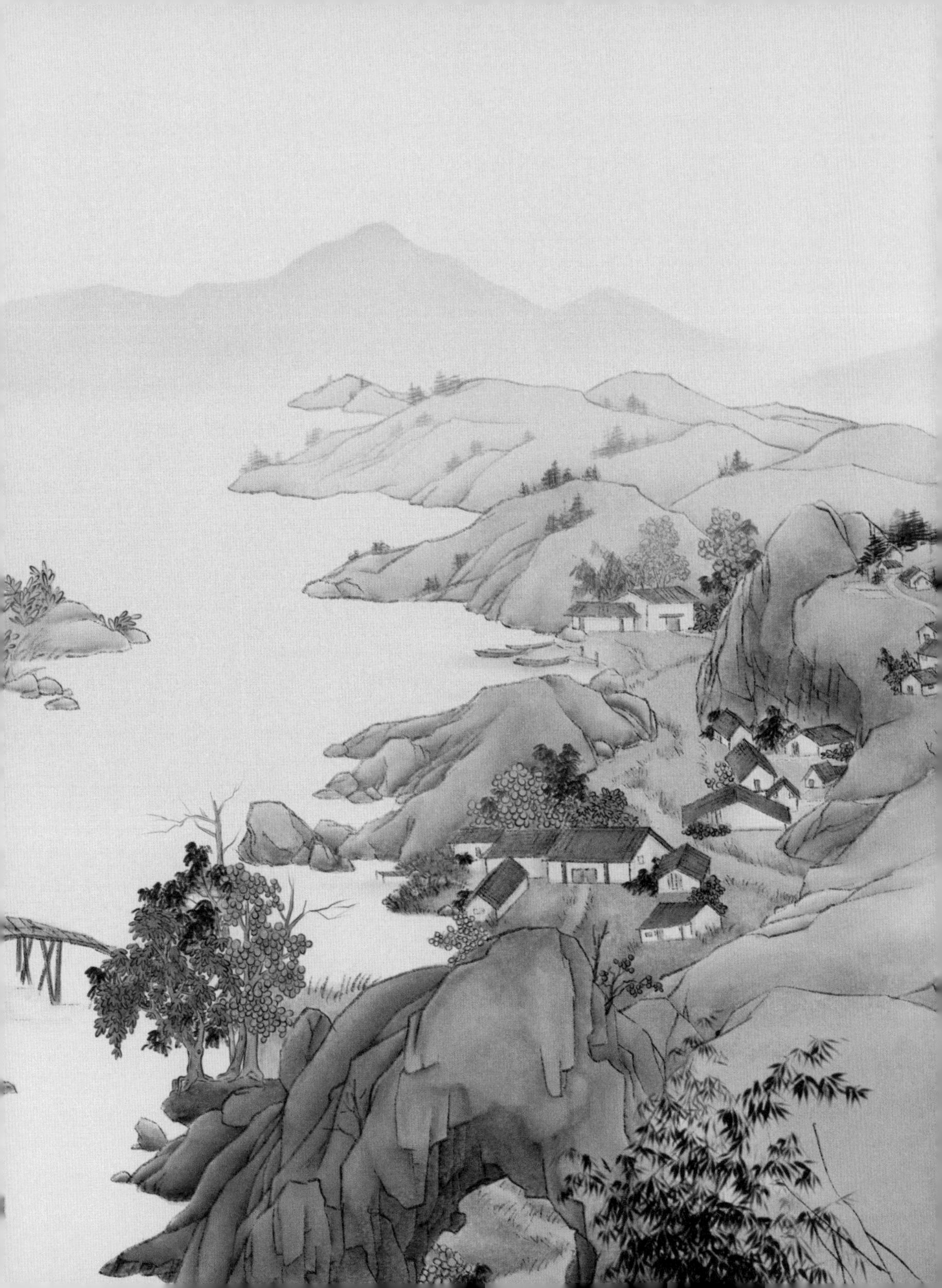

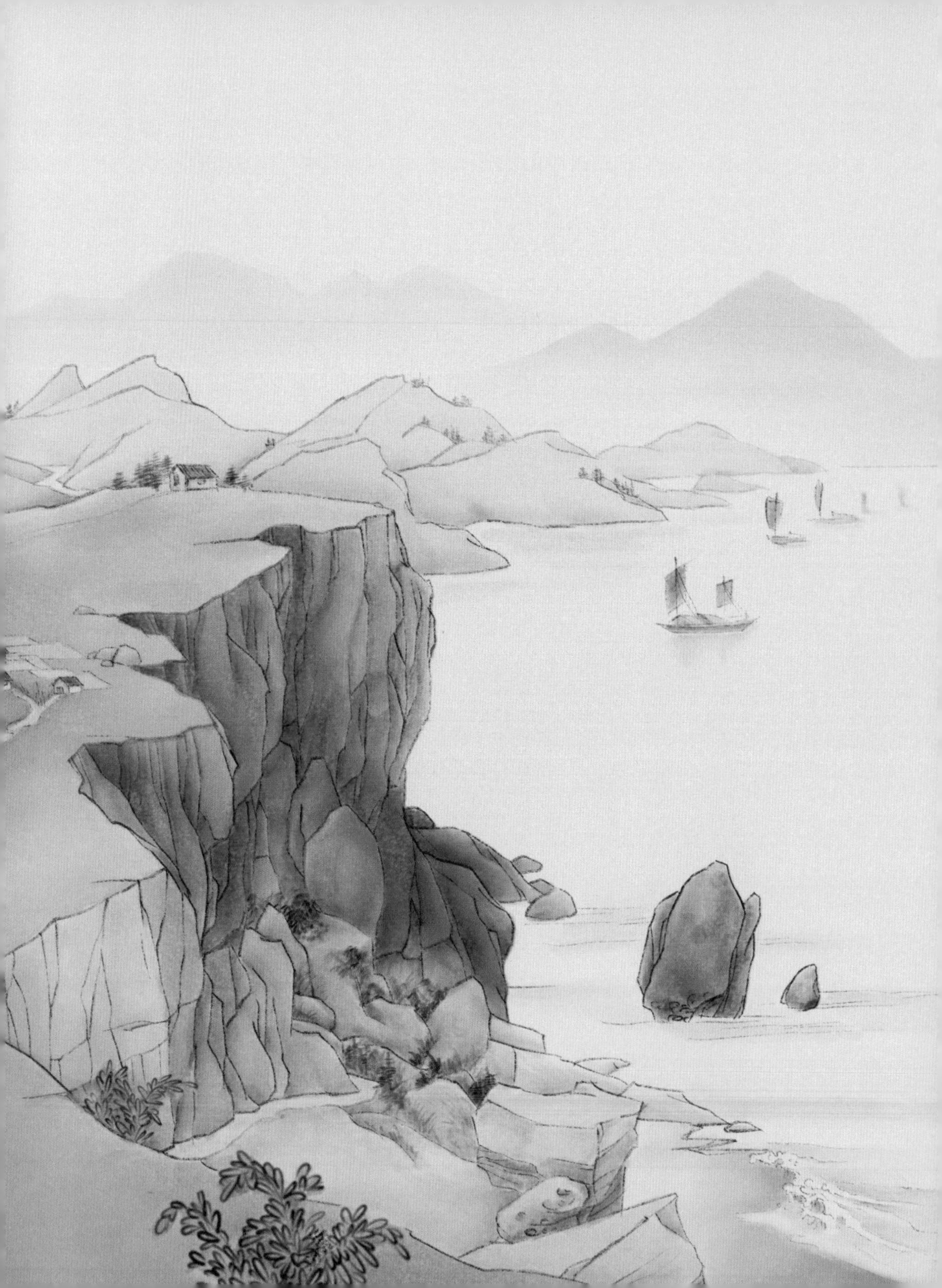

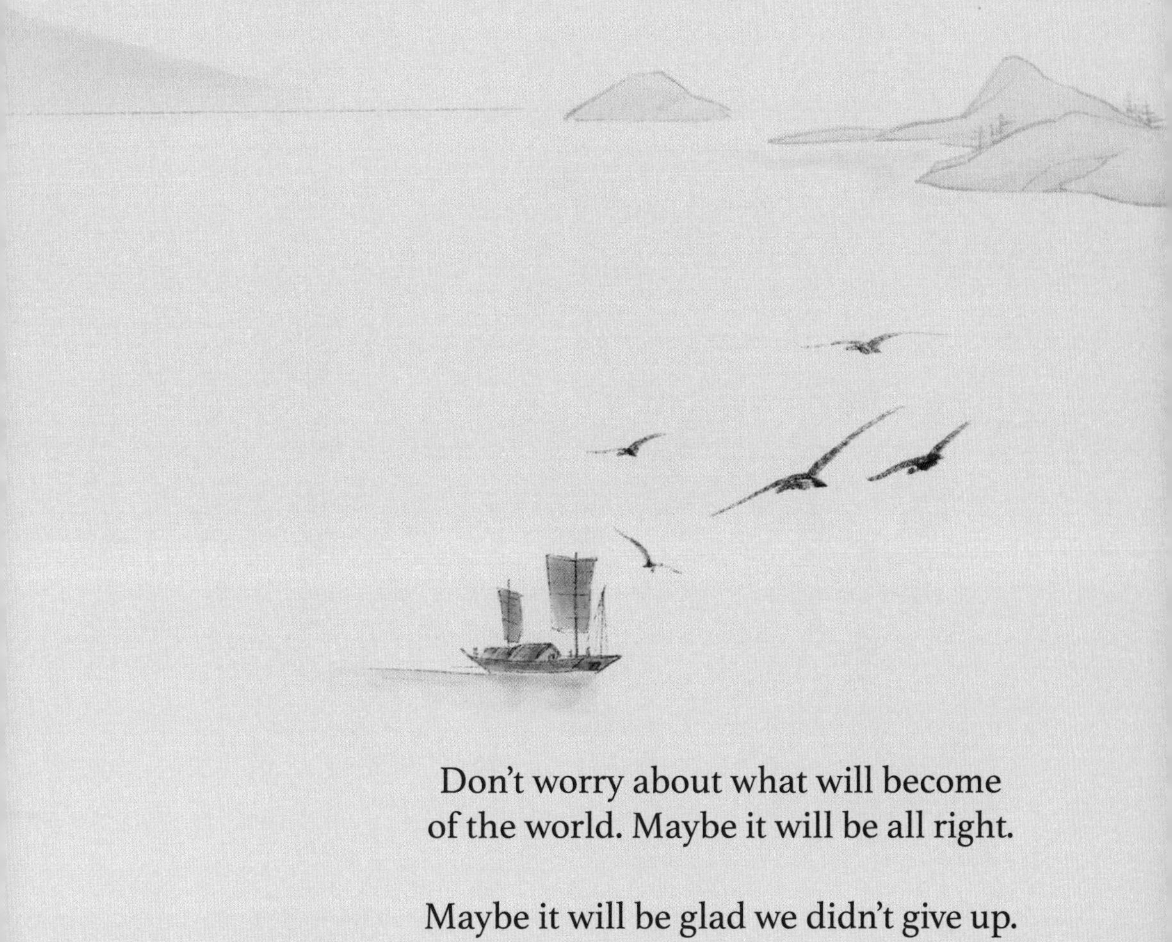

Don't worry about what will become
of the world. Maybe it will be all right.

Maybe it will be glad we didn't give up.

"Did you know that the whole
world is inside a tiny, tiny drop?"

ACKNOWLEDGMENTS

Though *The Oxherd Boy* finds its roots in ancient Chinese philosophy, it wouldn't exist without the supporting river of contemplative wisdom that flows through multiple traditions, both old and new. From Hindu spirituality, Stoic philosophy, and Sufi poetry to modern Western psychology and the works of thinkers, writers, and illustrators of our time, whose characters continue to touch the hearts of readers everywhere, thank you all for showing me how the world thrives when we make space for love, compassion, and community every day.

The internet is a strange place to hang out sometimes, but I'm grateful to Google Maps, Instagram, Facebook Groups, and Twitter for bringing me together with everyone who shaped

The Oxherd Boy from the start. Thank you to Zheng Zhi-Hong, for agreeing to teach me the ancient painting traditions and encouraging me to move on from them. To the Oxherd Boy online community, it's been an unspeakable privilege to be invited onto your screens and into some of the most tender recesses of your lives. To Sam and Liz, thank you for reading my half-baked writing and choosing to explore the possibilities with me.

Thank you, Lindley, Angelin, Danielle, Luisa, Bridget, and the Penguin Random House team. I can't express how grateful I am for your farseeing eyes and guiding hands that held this book through every moment and brought it to life so beautifully.

Thank you, Mommy and Daddy, for letting me explore who I am and smoothing the way for my more worldly worries while I learned how to make passable paintings.

Thank you, Damian, for being both my most humbling teacher and my most faithful student. Do you want to be dogs?

Thank you, Ben, for listening. Always listening. For being my dance partner through this most incredible time together. There are no words but gratitude and joy. Okay, okay, I'll let you stretch now.

To all the friends, family, strangers, supporters, and critics, whose presence has been a well from which I drink daily, thank you.

REGINA LINKE is a Taiwanese American artist specializing in contemporary Chinese *gongbi* painting, an ancient form of brush painting that depicts narrative subjects in colorful high detail. She enjoys writing and illustrating stories that celebrate East Asian folklore and philosophy in an accessible and modern way. She lives with her family in Rhode Island.

Published in the United States by Clarkson Potter/Publishers, an imprint of the
Crown Publishing Group, a division of Penguin Random House LLC, New York.
ClarksonPotter.com

CLARKSON POTTER is a trademark and POTTER with colophon is a
registered trademark of Penguin Random House LLC.

Library of Congress Cataloging-in-Publication Data
Names: Linke, Regina, author, illustrator.
Title: The Oxherd Boy : Parables of Love, Compassion, and
   Community / Regina Linke.
Description: New York : Clarkson Potter, 2024.
Identifiers: LCCN 2023009125 (print) | LCCN 2023009126 (ebook) | ISBN
   9780593580547 (hardcover) | ISBN 9780593580554 (ebook)
Subjects: CYAC: Fables. | Oxen—Fiction. | Rabbits—Fiction. | Conduct of
   life—Fiction. | LCGFT: Fables.
Classification: LCC PZ8.2.L465 Ox 2024 (print) | LCC PZ8.2.L465 (ebook) |
   DDC [E]—dc23
LC record available at https://lccn.loc.gov/2023009125
LC ebook record available at https://lccn.loc.gov/2023009126

ISBN 978-0-593-58054-7
Ebook ISBN 978-0-593-58055-4

Printed in China

Editor: Angelin Adams
Editorial assistant: Darian Keels
Designer: Danielle Deschenes
Production editor: Bridget Sweet
Production manager: Luisa Francavilla
Prepress color manager: Neil Spitkovsky
Copyeditor: Mi Ae Lipe
Marketer: Joey Lozada

10 9 8 7 6 5 4 3 2 1

First Edition